Glassball Art Projects

Mountsorrel Arts and Heritage Project

Memories of Stone, Steam and Steel

First Published 2012
by Glassball Art Projects
www.glassball.org.uk | info@glassball.org.uk

Compiled by Glassball Art Projects
Book design by Cora Glasser
Production Management by Geoff Barlow
Printed and bound in Italy by Graphicom

Cover image is of the 'Sky tip' at the No.1 quarry, courtesy of Lafarge
Back cover image is of the stonework at the new Learning Centre, The Green, Mountsorrel
Frontispiece by Fran Mills, taken during a visit in 2011 to the Mountsorrel quarry (Buddon Wood)

This project was kindly supported by The Heritage Lottery Fund | www.hlf.org.uk

ISBN: 978-0-9558060-4-9

Contents

I was born in Mountsorrel on 20th December 1934 and went to our local schools and, apart from my RAF service, I have lived, married and worked here, or nearby, all my life. I have always taken a general interest in the village.

The local quarries are particularly important to me because of having three generations who worked for the quarries: my great-grandfather, Jacob, who was an engineer there; my grandfather, George, he was a locomotive driver, driving Doris I & II (that was the name of locomotives that he drove for many years); and my father, who was a joiner there, but he ended his working life there in charge of the maintenance on the general equipment throughout the quarries. So it's been quite an interest to me to gradually pick up the information in relation to the quarries. Some of it I've been able to read about, but the bulk of it has come from my father, who was very good at talking about his work because he loved it; his work was his life. He really enjoyed the work at the quarry, building new equipment, maintaining the equipment. It was a dirty job, and of course during

the cold weather you couldn't have had anything much colder than a quarry, but he did enjoy it and he was highly thought of by the management.

Leicestershire is a county of considerable beauty, with its undulating countryside and forestry, especially the Charnwood Forest, where tourists come from far and wide to picnic and view the bluebell woods and its wonderful surroundings. In our village of Mountsorrel they could climb the hill where a medieval castle once stood, looking over the Soar Valley.

These beauty spots have been home to quarrying going back to Roman times, both for slate and hard rock. In 1876 the Mountsorrel Granite Company took over the rights and workings of the Broad Hill quarry from the executors of John Martin. The number one quarry, which operated from our village and which stands on the edge of the Charnwood Forest in the Soar Valley, produced the famous pink stone, for road building, paving, monuments, housing etc. Most famously, granite from the quarry was applied to the forecourt of Buckingham Palace, unfortunately now covered over by tarmac. The old number one quarry became a landfill site, and now has sheep grazing, and a new footpath with seats. The new quarry, as we will call it, is now owned by Lafarge Aggregates & Concrete UK, producing millions of tonnes of stone per year and is the largest granite quarry in Europe.

Mountsorrel is called a town because we had an annual fair, granted to us by Nicolas de Seagrave in 1292, but I still continue to call it a village. The village had many companies, some large, some small, all of which played a significant part during the war years. The Mountsorrel Granite Company, Rolls-Royce, Alvis, Clarke's Boxes, Auster Aircraft (Repair Shop), Boot and Shoe manufacturers, leather board mill, industrial laundry, knitwear, elastic webbing, The War Agricultural Department, to name but a few. Our local bus garage (Allens Blue Buses) supplied a single-decker bus fitted out as a mobile first aid unit (called 'The Mobile Post').

The Home Guard used part of the Granite Company ground for training purposes and a lookout post on top of the waste tips (called 'The Seven Sisters'). Their meeting place was the WD Drill Hall, built in 1901 at the North end of the village. Just down the road, in Quorn, a Military Camp was built for the Pioneer Corps, later the American 82nd Airborne, prior going to war in Europe.

When the Americans were encamped at Quorn, us youngsters would stand on the roadside when convoys of their lorries were going by and shout 'Any gum, chum?' They would throw down field rations containing biscuits, chewing gum and sometimes cigarettes.

One of the most significant sights in Mountsorrel and still standing today is the War Memorial on top of Castle Hill, once the site of a medieval castle (1080–1217). This memorial was built by the Mountsorrel Granite Co. in 1926, with a plaque on one side with names of the men who died fighting during WW1, and on the other side, WW2. For many years the armistice service was held here in November each year.

Volunteering in Mountsorrel is very strong. At the bottom of the village green, due to a few dedicated volunteers, a Youth Café has been formed, with a youth worker giving the young people some incentive to get involved in various activities. The Heritage Group formed a year or two ago is gaining ground, and also a disused mineral railway line, once part of the Mountsorrel Granite Co. is in the final stages of restoration due to the massive input of dedicated volunteers.

Working with Glassball Art Projects, members of the Mountsorrel Heritage Group, including myself, were keen to get the younger element of the village involved, and older people too, to record their views and recollections by interviewing friends and relations about their lives and works etc., gaining in the process a greater understanding of Mountsorrel's unique history. A number of publications have been produced over the years on the village, but I am sure this one, with its stories from local residents, will give you a new insight into the village. It has been a pleasure to have been involved, and the interaction with the residents, young and old, ready to pass on their views and listen to what you have to say, has been very valuable to this project. I am sure it will bring back a lot of memories of things that people will have forgotten, or enlighten them of what has been. We know the clock can't be turned back, but the people who have come to live here, and visitors, say what a friendly place it is.

Noel Wakeling
Member of the Mountsorrel Heritage Group and
long-term resident of Mountsorrel Village

Long-term residents of The Yard by The Green (on the left Miss Sarah Dodge with her mother), image courtesy of Mary Geary (Nee Lovett)

Back in 2009 Glassball Art Projects completed an innovative arts and heritage project, titled *Stories of Stone*, working with the young people of Sterndale Moor in the High Peak of Derbyshire. The project was to investigate the working lives of the local quarry workers who were employed by the many limestone quarries in this part of Derbyshire, the hamlet of Sterndale Moor being originally built in the 1930's to house such workers. During our time with this unique community we had the chance to talk with employees at Dowlow quarry, which is owned by Lafarge Aggregates & Concrete UK. The resulting *Stories of Stone* publication was well received, along with a well-attended exhibition at the Buxton Museum and Art Gallery.

We were pleased to receive a call from Angus Shedden, the former Quarry Manager at Mountsorrel, to say that Lafarge would be interested in supporting a similar project at their site next to the village, and in partnership with the Mountsorrel Heritage Group, which had newly formed. Many meetings later and with a funding application under our belts, we were very lucky to receive the news that the Heritage Lottery Fund was keen to support our new arts and heritage project in the village. The project was expanded to cover not just the quarrying industry, but other major industries that have worked out of Mountsorrel.

So work began in earnest in 2011 with volunteer training, film and photography workshops, oral history training, quarry tours, photography trips, open days, and much more. Over thirty interviews were recorded during the course of the project, with many areas of Mountsorrel life being covered; more than the original project had set out to record. The contents of this book represent a selection of what the project group discovered over the course of a year. The following texts are extracts from the many interviews that took place, and were transcribed verbatim. It is not to be viewed as an academic account of the history of Mountsorrel and its connected industries, but more as a series of recollections, glimpses, tales and experiences that are all rooted in this wonderful community.

This book and accompanying exhibition would not have been possible without the tireless enthusiasm and commitment of the project's volunteers, young and old. Glassball Art Projects would like to thank Anne Hickley at Penguin Office Services, the staff at the Mountsorrel Learning Centre, Colin Hyde from the East Midlands Oral History Archive, Leslie Strange and volunteers from the Mountsorrel Youth Café, Leicestershire County Council, Peter Osborne (former Chairman of Leicestershire County Council), staff at Lafarge Aggregates & Concrete UK, Tina Ball, and Amanda Turner at the Heritage Lottery Fund. Thank you also to our young volunteers, in particular, Fran Mills, Katy Ivison, Chloe Foster, Amber Van Der Vloet and Claire Morgan, who took part in the project and helped capture Mountsorrel's local distinctiveness for future generations.

A special thank you to Angus Shedden for instigating the project, providing transport and supervising the many quarry visits, and for providing valuable access to archival material stored at the Lafarge Mountsorrel offices. Our special thanks must go to all the adult interviewees for allowing us to record their memories and share with us their many precious photographs. We are very grateful to all the members of the Mountsorrel Heritage Group for their continued support throughout the project, in particular Keith Foster who helped us stay well connected with Mountsorrel life. And finally, we are indebted to Noel Wakeling for his gracious support and wonderful knowledge of all things Mountsorrel.

Cora Glasser
GAP Project Coordinator

'At night one could watch the lights of vehicles on the ceiling, the A6 was getting busy then, and hear the sound of steam trains across the valley, long slow clinking trains of mineral wagons.'

Robin Davies

I must have been about 12 or 13 and it was winter time, the early 1950's, I can't give you the exact year, and Hawcliffe Hill Quarry had a lot of water in it because they used to have a washing plant at the top and they used to pump the water out to wash the gravel and sort it out, and this particular winter time the water had frozen down in the quarry and we as lads, because it was on two levels, there was the water, up the quarry, on to another level. And we were on that second level and we thought, 'Yeah it's a good idea if we get some of these boulders and roll them down about 80' down into the quarry to smash the ice.' And the ice must have been quite thick; all I remember was some of them not breaking it but we broke it in the end, great fun breaking all this ice, terrific. And in the night it snowed and so it covered the quarry over. Now Pat and myself went up the next morning to see where we'd broke the ice and you couldn't see it and we walked from where the incline was down right across the water, right across the ice to where we thought it was, and we were sort of padding around trying to feel this ice

breaking and I found it and I went straight down. And as I went down I put my hand up and Pat pulled me out, but what I'd got on was wellingtons and I'd got a set of blue overalls which I wore at school for the engineering shop where we did metalwork, and if I'd have been in there five seconds longer the wellingtons would have filled up and they would have gone down and I would have gone down like a stone. And I was in and out in about 10 seconds flat and I daren't tell me dad when I got home, he'd have killed me, absolutely killed me, so I said we'd been down Betty Henser's Lane and there was a pond in one of the fields and we were playing on the ice there and it had broke through and I fell into it, so that was the explanation I gave my dad. But yes, that was Pat Whelband saved my life a long, long while ago, but I'm always grateful to him, bless him.

At 14 one of the things you started to do was going to learn to dance at The Reading Room in Mountsorrel, we used to have a Wednesday night dance for all the village. And Harold Widdowson used to run it, him and his wife, he used to work at

Mountsorrel Market Place, property dated 1677, image courtesy of Margaret Manning (Nee Burton)

the quarry and he lived in the company cottages. On a wind-up gramophone, a 78 record, you learned to dance there. You used to have a cup of tea and that at half time and I think at the age of 14 I had my first half pint of beer in The Railway pub across the road, and it was good. And we joined the youth club, the Mountsorrel Acorn youth club with Harold Newman. I was in that and in actual fact I took my wife there, I took my young lady there who later became my wife, started courting her when I was 20 and I was at the youth club for about six or seven years, quite enjoyed it, had some good times at the youth club, great, absolutely great.

I've got a lot of memories, obviously lots of memories. I mean in the '60s it became a very dirty village because all the quarry traffic was coming through the village, you can imagine the dust and debris that used to be along the A6 and it got really run down. I'm pleased to say I've been living back here now for ten years and it's a hundred times better than what it was, much cleaner and much nicer now because we've got Granite Way there and it's all superb and

you know Mountsorrel is trying to lift itself up now. It's nice, it's quite a nice village. I've always enjoyed living here, it's been brilliant and where we are now it's superb. Ideal.

Butter Market (Dome), built in 1793, Tina Ball, 2012

Margaret's father, image courtesy of Margaret Manning

Margaret Manning (Nee Burton)

My Dad [Frank Burton] was a gardener you see and he used to send his stuff to Leicester market and she'd been in shop work and I can see my granny sitting in that front room watching this house going up and saying, 'You silly old fool; why send your stuff to market off this big piece of land when I can sell it for you in the shop!?' He would never go in the shop. So it was built, it's got a front room and a shop front. I don't think it was converted, I think it was halfway built when they had it done and they had it as a shop and they sold everything; they didn't just sell the greengroceries, they went into grocery as well and during the war I used to have to count the coupons because my dad had gone in the army and my granny had died in 1942 and I was only a little tot. And then later on they bought this other piece of land, it's all built on now. It was because there was allotments down the side and there was going to be no access because the other roads all came up to the bottom of it, and you can still visualise how it was. Anyway, they had all this land and they had hens as well. My grandpa had pigeons, he had racing pigeons, and thereby hangs another little story because he used to race these pigeons and they had a friend who raced pigeons and he said, 'Oh my pigeons are a lot better than yours.' And my grandpa said, 'Oh well,' he never argued, he said, 'Well, we'll see.' So they took these pigeons to somewhere to race back again and this other chap's pigeons never came back!

The Foulds family, image courtesy of Margaret Manning

This is Edith Mary and my granny and Edwin Foulds, gardener and seedsman. That's her father and her mother; I know all about them. And these are different censuses that I've done you see. I was going through the censuses and I found the Foulds, you know, the various places where they'd lived through the village and then I was looking and I was looking for 'Foulds' and I couldn't find her and I realised her name was Perkins because she'd got married you see, and she lived on The Green up here somewhere at one stage and she must have been poor because she took in a lodger, Daniel Perkins. This is the whole family. So at that stage she was married and she'd got a brother and a sister both living with her. She had a shop on the Cross apparently. Everybody says 'Mrs Baggley's shop', I don't know, I don't remember Mrs Baggley's shop but that's what a lot of people say. Well it was alright for a start off. I think when we went to the shop it was a bit chaotic really. I was an only one but, you know, I wasn't pushed into the background but the shop had to carry on being run, so I had to go with it, so to speak. So I helped by counting coupons and I used to pick gooseberries and things like that and we had a German prisoner of war that helped out a little bit as well at one time but the garden was left really; we used to sell cut flowers as well, so I used to cut them.

I lived at the shop, until 1961 I think it was, when we sold it. From 1942 there was no electricity laid on when we went in there and my mother said, 'I'm having electricity!' Now that was very difficult at that time because you couldn't get the electricians or anything, so everything was done on the black market.

Outside my parents shop (Margaret nearest to camera), image courtesy of Margaret Manning (Nee Burton)

JW Porter & Son Haulage Contractors, image courtesy of Kay Valentine

Kay Valentine (Nee Porter)

Mum she's from Leicester, but my dad, he's been in Mountsorrel, well he was, in Mountsorrel all his life. They used to live in Sileby Road, they lived, I don't know where else they lived actually, I think it was mainly Sileby Road, they had taxis at that time as well as the lorries, but the lorries have been around since the 1920's. So it's been a Mountsorrel family, well since about the 1500's I think if not before, and they also moved up to Rothley and there used to be a garage on Rothley crossroads at Rothley house and grandpa designed and built that.

He was an entrepreneur, he'd do anything and everything, but it was in the 1930's design and I think there was a lot of trouble when they wanted to pull it down because of the actual building, it was a bit sort of deco I suppose, it was lovely. And they lived on Croxton Top, they had a big house up there when we were children, we lived up there, which was absolutely lovely, but the business has always been based in Mountsorrel. And where we lived at the corner of Crown Lane when mum and dad were married and all us children came along, grandpa wanted to build on the farm at the back because that was all his and the dairy and everything therein, he wanted to build a garage and three bungalows for his daughter and two sons, but because of the quarry workings he wasn't allowed to do it. So the garage stayed on the main road just down from Crown Lane.

It was too close to the quarry because the property went right up Crown Lane and as you come round the top you've got the quarry right at the top, so obviously in those days when they blasted

Mountsorrel Gala, image courtesy of Kay Valentine (Nee Porter)

the granite came right down onto the main road, sometimes anyway! I know grandpa had a few pieces that had come down there and we didn't realise that blackberries were black until we were about 15 because they were just a very nice pale pink, you know, from all the granite dust. And we used to play up there, we used to play on the tips and everything. Redlands used to help every year with the parade

through the village, the summer parade, and we used to have a big do on The Green and all the stalls and everything. And I believe they've done quite a lot actually in the village.

Noel Wakeling

Well I've lived here all my life and we lived in Hawcliffe Road, No. 6 and then moved to 44, around about 1938, which subsequently became our family home up until me leaving to go into the services. Well my family background, my grandparents were farmers at Swithland but my father was a joiner and an engineer with the Mountsorrel Granite Company and where he worked all his working life. My grandfather, my father's father, George Wakeling, he worked for the Granite Company too and he'd been a locomotive driver with the Granite Company driving Doris I & II, that was the name of the locomotives, and he drove them for many years.

George Wakeling working on the Peckitt Loco Doris II, in No.1 quarry, image courtesy of Lafarge

I was always extremely active as a child and although I didn't partake as I got older in any of the sports like football, rugby, I did play to some extent cricket, but not on a regular basis, with Mountsorrel Town Cricket Club. I did enjoy going to school all the while. I never, ever, didn't go to school because I didn't like it. I did enjoy going to school and I got on pretty well at school. I started at Christ Church in Mountsorrel for which the head mistress at that time was a Miss Bailey, and she was my grandmother's next-door-neighbour and so I always used to think that I was probably a bit privileged there although I never was, but you know you did feel that as a youngster, you thought you'd got one over on your friends because the head mistress lived next door to your grandma. I enjoyed my schooling and then the time came when we left Christ Church, moved down to St Peter's and I was there until of course the time when I went to Humphrey Perkins and it was, funnily enough someone asked me the other day how we used to go to Humphrey Perkins and did you walk, did you go on a cycle or did you go on a bus? Well in those days there used to be a bus service from Quorn called

Howletts and they used to pick the Mountsorrel children up and take them to Humphrey Perkins and bring them home in the afternoon. Although I did go by cycle when the weather permitted and we used to cycle down Betty Henser's Lane as they called it, there was no bypass there as there is today, and go across the fields and out up Mill Lane at Barrow-upon-Soar and then on to the school.

My father, being a joiner, always wanted me to follow in his footsteps and be a joiner. I must say that I rather do like woodwork and I've done quite a lot of it but my main ambition was the motor trade, I did like cars and that sort of, I always lean towards that side of things, something mechanical, and so yes, that's the way I went into the motor trade, which then of course, that took me up to joining the Royal Air Force.

Michael Griffiths

Born in Mountsorrel at the former vicarage, then a nursing home (now the Mountsorrel Hotel on Loughborough Rd.), I was baptised at St. Peter's

St. Peter's Primary School, image courtesy of Patricia Tomkins

Church of England and went to the Christ Church Infants' School, then St. Peter's Primary School (at Watling Street above the Butter Market). I lived in Mountsorrel until 1965 when I went away to university.

My mother's ancestors included families from Mountsorrel with the surnames Twigg, Gee (or Jee) and Paget, which I've traced to the 18th century in church registers (the village was then divided between Rothley parish (the South End) and Barrow parish (the North End)). An ancestor, Thomas Twigg (early 19th century), lived in a cottage on The Green where the library now stands (in between it was the location of the Church Hall). He was a framework knitter and the pound keeper. Stray animals were kept in an enclosure (the pound, poundfold or pinfold) at the top of The Green. Framework knitting (hosiery, gloves) was a major occupation, carried on in people's homes or maybe small workshops. My mother (Betty May Nix; 1922-1988) was born in Plymouth and came to the village as a child to live with her aunt.

My mother and her second husband (Frank Griffiths, 1923-2001) both worked at various times at the Rolls-Royce plant in Mountsorrel: my first memory of her work is of her in a white coat as laboratory assistant in the radiography lab at Rolls-Royce. We lived in a number of houses in the village. My mother also had a number of clerical jobs (at Rolls-Royce, at Fisons and at Trent in Loughborough). For some years they owned a guest house on Loughborough Rd (at the corner of Hawcliffe Rd and Loughborough Rd, the north side) – now replaced with another building.

I was an only child. My mother and I first lived with my widowed great aunt, Rosetta King (formerly Nix, 1880-1961), at Roecliffe Cottages, 176 Loughborough Rd, an end terrace with three storeys, six rooms and a cellar, built in 1882. The top floor was used as an attic and was full of all kinds of fascinating junk such as a defunct pinball machine and a union jack used to celebrate the Relief of Mafeking in the Boer War. There was an outside WC and a coalhouse, and a range of brick sheds for tools and bits and pieces. In the garden at one time was a chicken pen (bantams kept once, I remember) and a vegetable garden. Also there was a hutch with rabbits, and an elderly male relative (Albert Seaton, 1878-1953) came when one had to be killed. Beyond the end of the garden was a field, part of the water meadows, with either mowing grass or cows, and a view down to the river.

The late 1940s and early 1950s was an age of austerity, recovering from the Second World War, so many things were rationed; and I remember my great aunt using her ration book at the butchers. Sugar was rationed, which meant sweets also, but kids generally had the benefit of adults' allocations. The state provided National Health concentrated orange juice to supplement children's diets. The general diet was limited in variety when compared to the present and mostly prepared and cooked in the home. There was a gas cooker but my great aunt still cooked some things on the small coal range. We had electric lights but the old gas lights were still in place in the front room. Outside, the street lights were small gas lamps (fairly dim). Water for washing was heated in kettles. Baths were in a metal tub brought out for the purpose. Water also had to be heated on the fire for washing clothes in a copper. Washing day (traditionally Monday) was a time of strenuous work therefore, and involved putting clothes and sheets through a mangle and hanging them on a line outside or drying them on a clotheshorse in front of the fire.

Winters were cold and damp. Floods in the fields along the river were regular and the water level rose in the cellar as well as the damp up the walls (no damp courses). The proximity of the river meant very dense fogs mixed with smoke from the coal fires. Pipes sometimes froze. The bedrooms were not heated, so hot water bottles were used. At night one could watch the lights of vehicles on the ceiling (the A6 was getting busy then) and hear the sound of steam trains across the valley, long slow clinking trains of mineral wagons. Working days were punctuated by the siren from the quarry. This sounded at the end of work and as a warning of blasting (there were also red flags near the quarries), and the blasting itself was felt as a dull subterranean thud.

Life was more locally-focussed. We knew quite a lot of people in the immediate area. A lot of shopping was in the village, though increasingly people went to Loughborough and (less frequently) Leicester by bus (there were several bus companies and a 20-minute interval service on weekdays). The village lacked many amenities (no dentist, optician, solicitor, limited banking, one café). Many people worked in home deliveries: milk, bread,

Aerial view of Mountsorrel looking south, showing Grand Union canal (left) & No.1 quarry (right), image courtesy of Lafarge

1860 'Echo' Bridge, carrying the Mountsorrel railway line to the main line at Barrow-upon-Soar, Tina Ball, 2012

groceries, papers, coal, bakery goods, and on some occasions soft drinks. Ice cream vans in summer. There were also rent collectors, school attendance officers, dustmen, postmen (twice a day and once on Saturdays), tramps, gypsies, a chip van, rag and bone men, window cleaners, chimney sweeps and a variety of salesmen.

For adults the numerous pubs were social centres. Because of its history Mountsorrel had many former coaching inns like 'The Grapes' (south of the Butter Market) that were converted to other uses (a shop in this case), but there were still many pubs open. There was a cinema (the Rock Cinema) south of The Green on Leicester Rd that I remember going to (though increasingly people went to Loughborough or Leicester for entertainment). Limited car ownership determined the range of travel and leisure opportunities.

School, as I remember it in these years, was traditional: spelling tests, times tables, reading and writing, arithmetic, all done soundly. There were also

PE, nature walks, music, art. Corporal punishment was still practised. I was able to go home for midday dinner on the bus but often one walked to or from school. My first teacher at primary school was Mrs Lane.

Children played outside a lot, roaming the streets, the hills and common, the edges of the quarries and the 'recce'. We were close to the river and constantly warned about it. Nevertheless we went to the 1860 bridge (the 'echo bridge') and the footpaths, towpaths and bridges, the lock, Jelly's Island, Betty Henser's Lane, the magazine with its small narrow-gauge trolley that you could ride on, and the withy beds. We would watch the weirs and the quarry railway to Barrow. There was a lot of foam frothing below the weir, with chunks floating in the air. This was caused by chemical pollution in the river (largely from Leicester). Looming above the village was a mountainous pink-coloured spoil heap, the 'sky tip', which could be climbed for an extensive view. We had an intimate knowledge of all the shops, and there were many small ones, especially the sweetshops, some very traditional ones with a great variety of jars of loose sweets.

Religion was in decline. Very few people we knew attended church regularly. There were some religious elements at school. Sundays tended to be rather dull, with shops closed, fewer buses, pub hours restricted, even big gaps in TV programming. Most people went to church only for weddings and baptisms, more rarely at Christmas or for funerals. However, the traditional year still had some life and the old festivals were remembered, mainly as holidays: Christmas, Easter (chocolate eggs), Whitsun, Harvest Festival (at school), Bonfire Night (fireworks easy to buy), and Pancake Day. As George Orwell suggests, the only religious moment that was widely observed was the two minute silence on Remembrance Day. There was a parade and wreaths laid at the Castle Hill memorial.

By the time I was 14 my mother had remarried and in the interim she and her second husband had a bungalow built where we lived for a few years before moving to 235 Loughborough Rd, (Hawcliffe House), which my mother ran as a guest house (initially with students from Loughborough Training College and later a bed and breakfast business). My stepfather still worked at Rolls-Royce, in the electrical maintenance section, then as safety inspector. The guest house was big, built in 1900, originally a gentleman farmer's residence and later occupied by a family named Peberdy, one of whom operated an electrical supplies business from an adjacent shop. It had a large garden and a range of outbuildings. I had a small bedroom at the front looking out across the valley to the distant Wolds. A line of steam in the distance showed the passing of trains on the Midland main line. This house was well built and had much more in the way of amenities: basically what you'd hope for today, though no central heating.

As well as the range of people at school there was an endless stream of customers at the guest house (commercial travellers, contract engineers, surveyors, drivers, cooks, tourists, students, from Britain and overseas) so I listened to many kinds of personal narratives while completing my homework. My mother had an additional business as a second-hand dealer. I used to go with her to public and household auctions. She would then re-sell purchases, usually to other dealers. The taste for the Victorian period was about to revive and there seemed to be a vast quantity of good-quality furniture, pictures, ornaments, and so on.

By this time I'd been on holiday to several regions of England and Wales, and to London, and because I had a bike I explored the local area, especially the Forest. So socially, geographically, imaginatively, and intellectually my horizons had expanded.

The Dedication of the War Memorial 15th August 1926,
(the two people sat together are Stanley Wakeling
in the Bowlerhat & his wife Gertie in the light coat),
image courtesy of Peter Hodson

We've had a lot of housing development here

There were fields when we lived up there but now there's big estates...

Mountsorrel Village: Then and Now

'Near to the old graveyard on the main road we used to have
a little sweetshop and that was more or less like walking into
somebody's front room...'

Project art work, by Katy Ivison, 2012

Aileen Lowndes

I'm amazed how the quarry has been fighting for the village. I live up on top of the hill and we've learnt to live with the explosions, you know, the blasting each lunchtime, so that we don't hear it, but it took a while to get used to it and especially when they have what they call the Mountsorrel smell. Well it was just that this, whatever it was, that had been dumped in there [former Broad Hill quarry was used as a landfill site], it was the most awful smell! I can remember it for one year any rate and it really was pretty bad.

Angus Shedden

Generally I think the quarrying industry is seen positively in the community. We're such a large employer and I think, particularly given the tough times that the country is going through now, I think that's seen as a real positive. We do try and provide funding and support for local events and donate materials for local schools and things like that, so I think generally we're seen as a positive influence on the village. I think without doubt there's always

room for improvement; we do occasionally have complaints about blasting or other complaints, and we work really hard to try and minimise our impact on the local community. I think anybody who comes to the quarry, when they first arrive at the quarry and actually see exactly what happens behind the closed doors almost, they're amazed at how much goes on, because generally the quarry is so well screened and because of the amount of effort that we put into minimise the impact that we do have.

For me the area that's changed the most is the area round Broad Hill and the area around where the old A6 offices are, and the reason I say that is because in our archives, and I've actually got photos on my office wall of that area when it was a quarry, and there is just dust and steam and smoke and railway wagons and all sorts happening all over the place. And then over time eventually that area, the quarry was finished and it's all been restored back to the Broad Hill that it was, and in addition to that the bypass that's been built has allowed all the quarry traffic which used to come out and go straight

Aerial view of No.1 quarry workings (locomotive sheds, crushing mills, power house, workshops & stores), image courtesy of Lafarge

Fair for quarry workers' families, image courtesy of Lafarge

through the middle of the village, all those wagons that used to trundle through the village now go out down Granite Way, which is a dedicated entrance road, and straight out onto the A6. That must have just totally transformed that part of the village and made it far more pleasant to live in.

Betty Berger

Well Mountsorrel has changed completely of course. It's no longer a village. It was very much because the quarry would be a very dangerous job, I mean people working within the quarry over the years and because quarrying was a dangerous job people tended to be a very close community. It's a bit like a mining village in the sense that it was a close community and we all knew each other and everybody, you know, they'd talk about so and so has got such and such a thing, you know we all knew who they were talking about. But then of course

Family portrait, image courtesy of Aileen Lowndes

when the war came Clarke's Boxes, which was up in the road up there, in Linkfield Road, they'd just started building a new factory and it was taken over by Rolls-Royce and so when they came of course what happened, they had to find accommodation for the work people that came from Coventry and things, and so they took, when I was a kid at school, where the school is now up there, all the rest up to those old houses was fields, paddocks and fields going right back to the quarry. And so it was fields and trees and things and so of course they started building on there and they built the roads, like Churchill Road and Martin Avenue, all these roads. And they brought in these prefab buildings, horrible little places they were, but they brought those in and all the families came to live there you see. And then they had the other buildings going down at the bottom as well you know, so they built those later. But of course when you get a lot of people moving into the village who don't belong here, that's what we see here. They think they belong here when they've been here a while but you know when new people move in it changes the atmosphere completely.

Claris Wignall

The new housing, well it changed the village you know. The Trees Estate, that was built for the Rolls-Royce, but Churchill Road and Martin Avenue, that was built for the Alvis when they came from Coventry. There was nothing there but fields.

David Taylor

My own experience is that once the company [Redland] becomes more open and there's a young lady who used to handle any complaints and she insisted it would be a lot better if we were more open and let people see what was inside, not try to hide it. And in fact I think against my idea, it actually proved to be the more people knew what was inside, the more they couldn't believe what we were doing didn't cause more problems.

Jackie Loughlin

We had some good times then and when I were younger I remember we used to do the Maypole down where, they're all houses there now, where the council offices are, at the back there. When I went

Mountsorrel quarry (Buddon Wood), Cora Glasser, 2012

to Sunday School, we used to go up to the memorial place and then we always used to go down to the fair. It weren't open but we used to have a service down there, I don't know why. Then we used to go to the youth club.

Let's see I were 15, it would be '59 wouldn't it [when I started at the box factory] and I worked there until I had the children. Yeah and then I went back part-time but then it got too much.

Oh dear, it employed a lot! Because you'd got Shepshed factory as well as the Sorrell factory, it were, you know where Rolls-Royce is, well it was at the side of Rolls-Royce. Up to a year ago there was, the factory was still there but then they demolished and built houses.

Mountsorrel's not changed down our end much, down the bottom end, but up the top end it's just expanded. It were all fields when we lived up there, but now there's big estates and that and in fact down where I live, they built all these houses at the back,

Clarke's box factory & new houses on the same site, top image
courtesy of Peter Hodson, bottom image David Ball, 2012

still building, and somebody asked me where the quay were. I said, 'The quay? I don't know where the quay is?' And it were at the back of us, it's q-u-a-y and I sent him off up the road somewhere! I thought, 'Well it can't be around here.' It's not changed, well apart from the traffic of course since they built the bypass, made it a lot quieter because it was just one row of traffic, but it is getting busier because they're building all these houses and now they've built the recycling centre. They said at the court, 'They won't come through the village, they'll go round on a bypass.' That's why I see cars going with all rubbish in them but it's not too bad at the moment.

The hospital? Well I remember that some of the men coming down the road and that, that some of them were a bit funny, well not funny but they used to have afflictions and that, and kids, you know what kids are like! But then we used to know this chap called, I think his name was Harry and his uncle had been in this Glenfrith for years and he came down to see us because he lived with his aunt and he came down and he says, 'My uncle's coming out of Glenfrith. He should never have been in there.' And he must have had a nervous breakdown or something and they used to put them in. The box factory, Keanes bought that land where Glenfrith hospital was and said they wanted it for a warehouse.

Phillip Proud

My grandmother died there [in the workhouse], that's a grandmother I didn't know, in 1930 she died. She was there because I got hold of this certificate not so long ago and it said she died at, I can't remember the address, a-hundred-and-something Loughborough Road, Rothley and I couldn't fathom out where it was. I were thinking, you know, in Rothley, but that was the old address of the hospital, it was Rothley, classed as Rothley because Linkfield Road, which used to be Union Lane, that used to be the boundary you see, but the hospital address was Rothley.

Kay Valentine (Nee Porter)

It's not a village anymore, there's not the closeness that we had, a lot of incomers who tried to reorganise a lot of things and in the end Mountsorrel people just faded into the background. It was like the gala and the fete, for a lot of years it was great but then suddenly some of the people who did it from Mountsorrel who passed too early really in years, it was never the same and it just faded. I don't know, the closeness has gone, that's all I can really say, it's too big; but having said that, I love the fact you can still walk up Halstead Road, you can still go onto the hills and you've still got fields. I'm just glad that they've turned down the building on Halstead Road, more building that they want to do, because when I was a child, that obviously was all fields.

There was a pub on every corner and I can remember a lot of them, you know, not because I drank when I was little but because they were still here. And also on the Butter Market we had the Co-op. We had three butchers on the Butter Market, we had a haberdashery, we had a bakery, we had the Co-op grocery store, Worthington's, a bank, yeah the shoe shop which was just down now where Pilbeam's is, we had a shoe shop there. We also had a cycle

Dinner Ladies at St Peter's School, May Porter (left) and Mary Hansen (right), image courtesy of Kay Valentine (Nee Porter)

shop, two or three newsagents, two chip shops, post office and this is all from The Green to The Green Bridge or to the Butter Market. Near to the old graveyard on the main road we used to have a little sweetshop and that was more or less like walking into somebody's front room, and then of course there was the sweetshop opposite where we used to live or just down a little bit where Paulson's used to be, another industry, and they had the mill onto the water. We had the cardboard factory in Linkfield Road, that was a big place. I know Linkfield Road you've got Clark's Boxes on one side and then the whole of the next side. I'm just trying to think what else there was because there used to be all houses down here on the main road where the garage is. Oh, of course, that used to be the bus garage, Allens Garage, and Mr Millner used to work there as well and they used to do all the transport for us going to school in Birstall, Allens Coaches and also for the runs to Skeggy every year, day trips to Skegness.

Linda Tyman
The council estate that is known, they call it the Trees

Estate; we used to call it the White City because it was white concrete houses, just over off Rothley Road at the back here. A lot of the people who lived on that estate were Rolls-Royce workers. For its time it was quite a big place. And more and more people were needed for that work so they recruited from round this area rather than just the people that had come from Coventry. Obviously, with the people coming here, they needed somewhere to live and in 1942 on Churchill Road some prefabricated bungalows were built and that's where my mother and her family lived. It was quite a change of environment because they'd been used to a city environment and all that offered and then to come to a bit of a backwater like this was a big cultural shock for them, I think.

The hospital used to be the workhouse and it was called the Barrow-upon-Soar Union. I don't know why it was called Barrow-upon-Soar, I suppose because Barrow-upon-Soar administered it. Barrow-upon-Soar Rural District Council was the local authority at one time. I don't know if it went back as far as when the workhouse was set up but

The Green in Mountsorrel (properties at the bottom were cleared for the building of the Memorial Hall), image courtesy of Peter Hodson

it was a grim looking place, as you can imagine, and when it stopped being a workhouse it became the Glenfrith Home for Mentally Disabled People, but that closed some years ago and a small bit of it remains that's been changed into bungalows. You can still see that bit, it's a one storey, it's called Rubicon Close, it's just off Linkfield Road. There's this piece of the original building that's been turned into private housing. But that's all that's left. It was quite a tall two or three storey building, very grim looking.

For us growing up it [the quarry] was always part of everyday life because you would hear the siren go when it was time for blasting and you would see the people walking to and from the quarry and it was only just where the Broad Hill is now, that was the quarry in my childhood. So it was very close to everyday life in the village, whereas now you wouldn't know it was there.

Mary Geary (Nee Lovett)
Mountsorrel is an industrial village, it's never been a pretty village, it's had lots of industry in it; the people are the salt of the earth. The community has lost some of its closeness since the developments we've had. It's a lovely village to live in and we've got some lovely walks, the river, Cufflin's Pit Lane, really nice walks, and it's a nice place to live.

I've lived here since 1964. I was brought up at Rothley, I was born in Mountsorrel, brought up as a child at Rothley, came as a young bride in 1964 to a cottage on The Green and I believe it's 47 years ago.

My mother and her family were all Rothley people who worked in the hosiery factory at Rothley, and they did things like seaming and linking and those jobs. My father was born in Newport, South Wales, his family were Irish immigrants. In 1930 the Depression came, he came to work in Rothley to build a bridge and met my mother and stayed. My grandfather was a farm labourer, my mother's father, he was, years ago, a groom at the Rothley Court Hotel when it was the Lord of the Manor's house, The Temple.

Tug of War, inter quarries competition (Mountsorrel won many), image courtesy of Lafarge

My home was a council house built in the 1930's, big, a large garden at the front, large garden at the back, we grew all our own vegetables and we had an allotment as well as did everyone else. People also kept hens. There was one fire in the living room, a coal fire, ice on the inside of the windows in the winter. There was lots of fields and spinneys to play in and pick bluebells and violets and primroses. The school was about three-quarters of a mile away, which we walked to, and the shops were, but it was a really lovely place to live, it was in a lane.

When I came in '64 the village was very, very dirty and dusty and lots of lorries rumbling through. The hosiery industry had a big impact, there was one or two hosiery factories and also the boot and shoemaking, there was one or two factories making boots and shoes and of course the big impact after the War was Rolls-Royce Aero Engines, that did employ a lot of fathers, sons and their sons and really a lot of people didn't need to go out of the village to work. There was the box-making factory, there was a factory in Halstead Road, I believe it was called the

Elastic Factory, and during the War apparently that made fuel tanks for Wellington bombers because a lot of the factories round here during the War had to revert to war work you see, they just had to change, but I believe most of the factories have gone now and it really has changed the village.

Well I've read a little bit about it [the workhouse] and I had an elderly neighbour who was born in 1900 and she used to say to me, 'When I'm old I don't want to go into the workhouse,' she still had that dread of that type of place. When it closed and it turned into Glenfrith Hospital for mentally disabled people who lived there and were nursed, because I can remember when I was at Rothley as a child they used to walk from Mountsorrel down the lane where I was living in twos, the men all together and the women all together and just used to go for a walk, that was in the 1950's, with a nurse at the front and a nurse at the back. It turned into the Glenfrith Hospital and also they had a big new part built on and they had a big kitchen there and the kitchen would cook the dinners for the school in the village because at that time the primary school never had a kitchen, so the dinners were cooked there. Then after it closed when the Mental Health Act was reviewed and it meant that the big institutions as it was were closing, they built two large bungalows in the grounds and they're in small units now with carers 24 hours a day, I believe that is right, and part of it was pulled down and new houses built on the site.

I believe the surrounding countryside has changed the most, the fields, they've been developed and I feel they've been over-developed, that's changed vastly, the marsh where the Jelson Estate is, and there's a lot of little corners of the village which were very scruffy and they've been filled in, like Little Lane at the back of the Parish Rooms, that was a boot and shoe factory and that's all been filled in with very nice houses. The Rolls-Royce site, that's all houses and also the big change was the bypass because it took a lot of the heavy traffic away and the fact that the quarry moved up to Buddon Wood and has got its own road, Granite Way, so the big

quarry lorries don't come rumbling through at six o'clock in the morning anymore and it's a lot cleaner. The houses along the main road, a lot of them were pulled down when we came, so that's changed, the character's gone, a lot of the character's gone, but it's cleaner than it was.

Well right near here the new library, which is absolutely splendid, the learning centre, that was a place called Twigs Cottage apparently, which was an old cottage up until the early 20th century, and then Christ Church at the top of The Green had a building put on there as their Church Rooms, it was called Church House and that was used for many, many years for functions for the church, Sunday school, coffee mornings, it was really used a lot, and then it kind of went into decline and I believe the church had to sell it. It was destined to be something not very good, I think possibly a builders' yard or something, but eventually I think Mr Antil took control of it and saved it and now we have the most wonderful library and learning centre, in keeping with the rest of The Green, and so it's good it's been saved.

Bond Lane double bridges, dated 1918/19, (some WW1 prisioners retained to complete construction), image courtesy of Patricia Tomkins

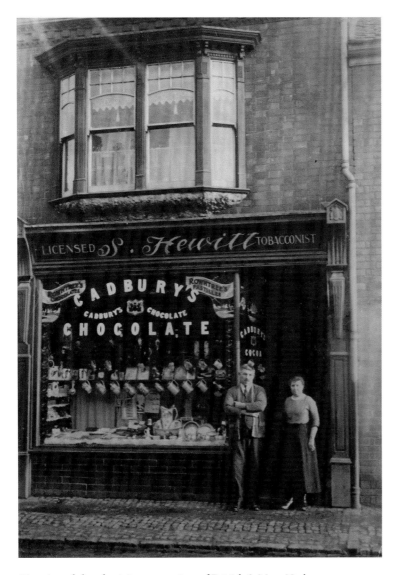

Mountsorrel shop front, image courtesy of Patrick & Mary Neal

Mary Neal

I moved here in 1955 because my father was going to work at Rolls-Royce, so we moved into what we called The White City then but now it's called The Trees, so it's Laurel Close, Elms Close.

I think Mountsorrel has grown too big because at one time you used to know everybody, you'd walk around and you'd know everybody and I think there was more of a community with people because we used to have gala days you know, and I can remember when I was courting Pat and we both dressed up and on the floats and things like this and we used to have them on The Green here. But then of course we had some trouble and they moved it up Halstead Road for a while and then people just weren't interested anymore so it just folded, but yes, it was good, we used to enjoy it and the kids used to dress up and things like that.

Maureen Henson & Jackie Woodier

MH: Yeah and then we went down to St. Peter's School and then I left there when I was 14 and had a year at Barrow Grammar, Humphrey Perkins, but we used to play, we used to play up the hills a lot, up the tips. I mean in them days, do you remember, probably you will, when we used to watch the train go across the railway? You know back down the village where the railway is? It went straight from the quarry and they used to grind it there and make all the fine gravel for the concrete slabs and it used to go straight through to Ellis's at Barrow.

JW: I remember my mum saying, she'd lie in bed in the mornings and she could hear the quarrymen's boots going to work before it was light because it was Mountsorrel quarry, that was Mountsorrel then. We used to go and play up the Common with jam sandwiches and a bottle of water all day. We had a cinema in Mountsorrel, we used to pay one-and-

something to go up in what they call the chicken run on Saturday afternoons, that's why we knew all the film stars, Alan Ladd, Clark Gable, and everybody smoked and if it went wrong everybody stamped their feet. We must just tell you about just down the road where that shoe place was, on the corner was a sweet shop called Polly Pope's and she used to have big boxes of sweets, not covered, in the window; she wore long black clothes, and all the cats, she had about four cats and they would be sitting in the boxes and you'd go, 'Could I have two ounces of jelly babies?' 'Yes me duck; get out!' Shoe the cats out!

The Grapes, Mountsorrel, Tina Ball, 2012

Christ Church Mountsorrel, circa 1844, image courtesy of Peter Hodson

MH: And then there was Mrs Harold just down the road at The Grapes, where The Grapes is. She was the little sweetshop and sold all sorts really.

JW: And then just further past where I live, there's Bennett's shop; now he's been there all my life but he's fishing tackle now, isn't he?

MH: When I were little it used to be Brooks's. Brooks's and then Mr Lake took it over and then Mr Lake he give it up; can you remember him with ginger hair? And then Bennett's took it on so I can remember the three lots. And next door to them was Mr Spence, the bike repair shop.

We used to have old radios, I bet you can remember this, the old radio where we used to sit and listen to Paul Temple and that, and all of a sudden it would go down, the radio would go down. We'd take the battery out, we used to call it an accumulator in them days and take that over to Spence's, bring the other one back, my dad used to connect it all up and we could listen to it again.

JW: I was born in Bond Street Maternity Home but I lived down there until I was nine. They knocked them all down, beautiful houses, and sold some of the land at the back. There were two wells because your Malcolm, he fell down one. So anyway the library was built on it and now that was moved to here at the Church House and this bit added on and then they've built more houses there.

MH: Mrs Fothergill lived there. Do you remember Mrs Fothergill who used to live there?

JW: No I remember the butcher.

MH: Goodwin's.

JW: And his sister lived next door doing hairdressing in the front room, because I used to go and scrub out for him on a Saturday lunchtime, I was only about six, I think he used to give me sixpence. And then there was Titcombe's, which was the hairdressers and is still a man's hairdressers now.

Looking up to the War Memorial on Castle Hill from the Butter Market, Tina Ball, 2012

MH: It's still a hairdressers but that used to be years and years ago a post office, do you remember that?

JW: No. It was Titcombe's all my life. And then we have Worthington's.

MH: And then it got sold, the post office moved up on Leicester Road and that's why they call where we live The Old Post Office Yard.

JW: That's right, and the house that I lived in is in the book of Mountsorrel that the Townswomen's Guild did, a very informative book, and my mum and dad's bedroom was a church window because it used to be a Methodist church. We've got no window in the kitchen; it was two-up, two-down.

MH: No we never had one in the kitchen, and them houses what we lived in, they was built in 1614, no sorry 1617. I can see it now, them houses.

I can remember when in Watling Street, his name was Mr Barnet, Billy Barnet and he used to bring the coal round on his horse and dray, and the coal, one day it was that heavy for the horse to come, its name were Daisy, I shall never forget it was a white one as well, a white, big horse. And one day it come round and it couldn't stop, the load were too much, it went straight through the Co-op window at the bottom!

JW: That was on that side of the road. This is all near the Butter Market.

MH: Yeah because on the Butter Market where Baron's Way is now, all down there, there was all shops, we'd got nothing but shops in this village. The saddlers, the Co-op butcher, the drapery, the Co-op itself and you could go round the back of the Co-op and there was a Co-op bakery round there and we used to go round and the loaves had just come out of the oven and me mum used to say, 'Will anyone nip across and fetch us a loaf?' The corners on the bread, when you came back there were no corners on it!

JW: Because you'd eat them! My mum was born

and bred in Mountsorrel but my dad actually came here with his parents because they were bombed out and they lived in Norwich and so they met down at Mountsorrel club and they got married in '43, February and I was born January '44 but he was in the RAF you see. And mum always used to tell this story, she's been dead for years now but she always used to tell the story that she used to put me across the road to the Co-op and Charlie Jackson the manager, he'd have the ration book and he'd tick the bacon that you'd had off with a pencil and I went over there one day and I said, 'Oh and it's no good you marking it off in pencil 'cause when I get home my mum rubs it out!'

Sue Selfe

I'll tell you what my memory of Mountsorrel is; not a particularly pleasant one but it was such a filthy place. You know when I was a child going on the bus between Loughborough and Leicester, not filthy in terms of rubbish lying around but from the quarry and, you know, the bus used to come this main road here, it was black. It was dusty. It was dirty. And now

I come back 40 odd, more than that, years later and it's nice, it's very nice. That road has made such a huge difference.

Robin Davies

Living at the top of Hawcliffe Road, I don't know whether anybody's mentioned this, there was a lot of tips there where they would tip the ballast in the past. A lot of them had got vegetation and had grown trees and that's where we used to roam, but there was one thing called the 'sky tip' and that was a huge mound of ballast which was about 200' high which had a road driven truck pulled up there by a winch and he used to just open his doors at the top and let all the ballast fly out and obviously if the wind was blowing, all the dust used to fly down Hawcliffe Road and it went on for 20, 30 years like that you know. And the dust levels must have been a lot worse than what they are now and nobody monitored those and I always remember mum complaining on Monday morning wash day if the wind was blowing the washing got dirty, stained and dusty. I remember that.

'Sky Tip' at No.1 quarry (used for depositing quarry waste & was over 200ft high), image courtesy of Lafarge

Peter Hodson

Oh yes there was a glove manufacturing and shoes, shoes where the Parish Rooms are now, that estate behind is on the site of an old shoe factory.

Well as you go from Rothley Road up Boundary Road, it was on the right hand side, there's some new housing, you can tell it's new because they're tiny and it was there. Every time a factory closes they knock it down and build houses like in Linkfield Road, they're building houses where the cardboard box factory used to be, and again where Rolls-Royce was it's all houses. The problem is that you get new people come in, move into those houses from outside, but all their work is outside the village, they've come from somewhere else, so their social life is elsewhere and really Mountsorrel is like a dormitory, just used for sleeping, and there's not a lot of feeling of village community and I probably get most out of the church and the heritage group.

Back in the 1980's there used to be a Carnival Parade each August for a number of years and they used to parade from Stonehurst Farm up to Halstead Road Playing Fields and that was quite fun and there was a number of local firms lent their lorries to use as floats and people dressed them up and I think people enjoyed that, dressing up the lorries and riding on them. The people who organised those, after a few years it became too much for them and there was no one coming on to take over from them I think that was the problem. There's not really a lot like that now and the nearest we get is the village charity fairs which we have twice a year.

Well the quarry was one of the largest employers at one time and at the top of the hill there, at the top of The Navins there's a house which at one time was a school for poor boys for Mountsorrel and Swithland according to the plaque on the side. And later on it became the hospital for the quarry workers and it's now a private house.

Up the road here at The Green, when you come to Christ Church you turn right, there's a no entry sign but you can walk up the hill and it's at the top of the

View from the War Memorial on Castle Hill, looking over the market place & meadows, David Ball, 2012

hill on the right. At the top of the hill, there's a walk past some cottages known as Castle Road, Castle Hill I think it's called. It wasn't a full-scale hospital I don't think, it was more somewhere to take them, more of a medical centre I think in modern terms we'd call it but in the 19th century I think they referred to it as the hospital for the quarry workers because it was dangerous work and there must have been quite a few injuries and it was somewhere to take them. Also if you go up by the scout hut there and follow the footpath up, that comes up to the same house.

Patrick Neal

Mountsorrel is not the place it was. It's grown out of all proportion. In the old days when you walked down the main street, you knew everybody, you'd say hello to everybody and everybody knew you, now you can walk through the village and not see a soul you know. The community, we used to have galas, we used to have garden fetes on The Green, the town band on The Green and if they do anything on The Green now, very few people come, only the locals or the people that are doing it and it's changed drastically. The employment has virtually all gone out of it because whilst the quarry's still here, it's so greatly automated, there's not the people here and it's basically a communter village, it's lost its heart, there's very few shops.

Rolls-Royce used to have dances every Saturday night and everybody used to have their dances at Rolls-Royce on a Saturday night, all the local companies, so you knew that if you wanted a night out on a Saturday night, you could go to Rolls-Royce and you could have a good dance, but now there's nothing, see, that's all gone. And there's not the factories really. When you walk round the village now, there's a lot of little industrial units, offices, and it's surprising how much there is but there's no big employers, only the quarry. Rolls-Royce have gone, all the big shoe factories have gone, the hosiery factories have gone, it's just really the quarry now and there's not that many work here for the size of the place.

Obviously we've had a lot of new housing. When I

Workers at Broad Hill quarry, image courtesy of Lafarge

Workers at Broad Hill quarry, image courtesy of Lafarge

was a youngster it used to start at the Main Street from the bottom end of the village near where Budgens is now, up to Rolls-Royce and basically it was The Green at Rothley Road, Churchill Road and one or two roads off, but now it stretches right over into Rothley.

We used to go to The Rock cinema when they used to have cinema up here, opposite the Alba Garage, that place that stands back, it's been a little engineering company; that used to be a cinema. They used to have The Rock cinema here and what was the one at Sowerby, The Futurist? At Sowerby? And they used to have one in Syston. And then as it got to the point where people stopped going to the cinema, and I can't remember when it would be, late '50's, early '60's, they started putting more films in a week to try and get people and then he turned it into a bit of a dancehall and he tried roller skating and it finally just closed. And I can always remember Bertie used to come round and if you were making a noise, he'd come round flashing his torch and he'd say, 'If you don't shut up I'll switch the bloody lights up!'

The Temperance Hall and the Old Reading Room which is next to bridge and has now been turned into houses. You know the bridge, if you go straight through that and immediately virtually at the side of the bridge there's a gable-ended building which is now a house or houses and that used to be the Reading Room and the quarry used to use that for the quarry parties. I can always remember that because obviously with my dad working at the quarry and we used to have these horses that you used to wind along and have horse races there.

Patricia Tomkins

There was pub, church, pub, chapel, all the way up the main road. And there were several you know, little avenues and apparently you could sell beer from your house. I think you needed a license but you could sell beer, you could make your own beer and sell it. And I know now there's still a house on Loughborough Road that you could go up the steps, go in the front room, knock on a little window that divides the two rooms and ask for a pint of beer. I mean you can't do it now but that, it's still there.

Clement Atlee visiting Mountsorrel, circa 1947/8, image courtesy of Mary Geary (Nee Lovett)

This is on the Loughborough Road and the number would be, I'll say number 57 Loughborough Road 'cause I lived at 61. 57 or 55 Loughborough Road. And up to so many years ago the glass was still in where you just knock on the window, and my great uncle lived there when I was a little girl as well.

The last house my grandma and granddad lived in was on what they called the bottom of the Rookery and they had my mum and my auntie. And my mum met my dad in the Railway, he was in the army and they got married and there was a house come up. In those days if you heard of a house that was empty you'd go and ask the landlord. And my mum heard that the house next door to her was coming up for empty and the landlord says, 'Yes, you can have it'. So my mum and dad started their married life next door to my grandma. So of course we were more in my grandma's than were at my mum's because my grandma had a television and we didn't, and then my dad would knock on the wall and say, 'Send her back round about half past seven' 'cause we used to watch, oh there were some frightening programmes

in those days I can remember, *Quatermass and The Pit*, I remember that and they was really frightening. And my mum had my sister, me and my younger brother. There were three children in one little tiny terraced bedroom with no bath, a toilet at the top of the yard and she put in for a council house. Well there wasn't many council houses in those days, I'm talking 1950s, and I was 11 when we moved. So stayed there till I was 11 and my mum got a council house up on what they called The White City which is now The Trees Estate and we moved up there. And then that was it, I was 11, the quarry, it wasn't my playground anymore.

I'd grown up, and that's the generations. But funnily enough when me and my husband got engaged, my uncle, the rich uncle, said, 'You've always loved living down Loughborough, haven't you?' I said, 'Oh yes, I want to go down there, live there'. He says, 'I'll buy the house for you' and he actually bought it, it was up for rent and then it was sold and put on the market and my Uncle John bought it for us and it was £1,100. We had a proper contract that we would pay him back every three months. And this sounds silly but every three months me and my husband used to go to his house in Stonehouse Avenue in Birstall and give him the money, the cash, I don't know how much it was, I don't quite remember. And then I'd write a letter, I wrote the letter, Dear, I think it was Straw & Pearce, Mr Morley of 58 Stonehouse Avenue has now been paid the rent, you know the mortgage, and that went on for seven years. So I went back to live in the house I was born.

Now after seven years me and my husband moved up to Cross Lane, just off the Rothley Road, the Cross Roads, bought a nice three bedroom semi-detached which I'm now there still. And my mum had a baby when she was 40, a late baby, and when he was about 19 he says to us all, 'I bought a house.'

Family portraits, images courtesy of Patricia Tomkins

'Oh have you?'

'Yes. It's on the Loughborough Road.'

'Oh what number?'

'Its' number 61.'

I said, 'Oh, that's where we all lived.' So my brother, not knowing because he'd been born up the council estate, he went down and lived there for seven years. My grandfather said when the floods were up you can go to the moon but you can't go to Sileby. Even now, the floods come up quite often down the lane and that's the only way you can get to Sileby. Unless you went to Quorn, caught a bus, went right round the back into Barrow and along. But say if you wanted to go to visit your auntie, 'cause a lot of Sileby people married Mountsorrel people so they were all your relations you see. My son lives at Barrow Road, Sileby, I can't get to him when the floods are up unless I go the long way round on the bus. We're in a valley you see. Me and my mum sat in the Waterside Pub a couple of weeks ago having a lunch and my mum was frightened because she knew the water was coming up over the canal and it comes, swirls round sometimes up to the pub wall, and I knew she was a bit worried about if the water comes up anymore, you know, but she's in a wheelchair and we'd have to push her through the water in a wheelchair.

Michael Griffiths

The workhouse building in Mountsorrel was the one built for the Barrow-upon-Soar Union (of parishes) in 1838-40 and was the place that a lot of destitute, sick, unemployed, disabled, vagrants and orphans were housed and fed in very basic conditions.

A lot of older people remembered this and had very negative feelings about it. I'm not surprised as in many ways it was part of a cruel, dehumanising system. When I was quite young someone read or summarised *Oliver Twist* to me, and I think this novel coloured my view of workhouses. Elements of the system persisted in unemployment payment practices and attitudes to the poor well into the twentieth century, and weren't entirely eradicated by the Welfare State.

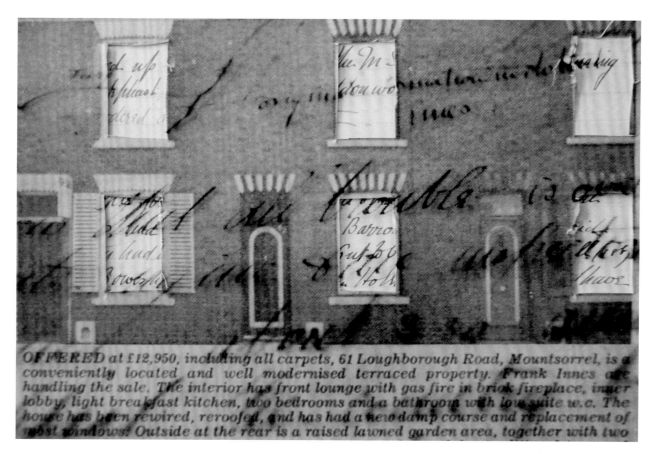

Project art work, by Fran Mills, 2012

VE Day street party in Mountsorrel, image courtesy of Patricia Tomkins

Rolls-Royce organised special trains annually via the Great Central line to Farnborough for the air show and we went several times. We went to Rutland once when the roads were difficult because of snow, via the Midland line. Apart from this I remember going to London and other places on the Midland line. We used the local trains (from Loughborough, Sileby, Syston) occasionally (for trips to pubs mainly); and on a few occasions I went to Derby and Nottingham from Sileby and Barrow.

I was last in Mountsorrel in 2002. The Rolls-Royce factory has gone. The bypass has reduced traffic flows to a degree, especially heavy vehicles, but the open spaces of the water meadows have lost a lot of their rural character. There are many more kinds of shops and services than when I was a child. What I noticed particularly were the new houses behind the existing ones along Loughborough Rd at the North End, and behind the buildings to the east of the Butter Market (all along the river floodplain).

Mountsorrel used to be very much a 'street village'

in form. Then the South End grew with post-war housing south of The Green. There's been a lot of infill building and building on subdivided plots of land. The access road to the quarry north of the village has changed that area. The river has got even more crowded with boats and moorings, but I was pleased to see the river access to The Railway pub. The Peace Garden at the top of Sileby Lane is interesting to me because there used to be a set of buildings surrounding an internal yard on this site, and this is where the Nix family lived when they first came to Mountsorrel in the late 19th century.

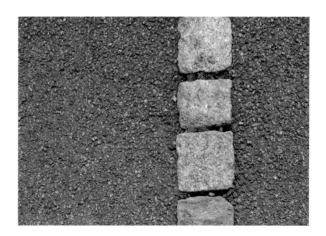

Granite setts, Cora Glasser, 2012

Castle Hill beacon, erected 1994 to commemorate 100 years of the Mountsorrel Parish Council, Tina Ball, 2012

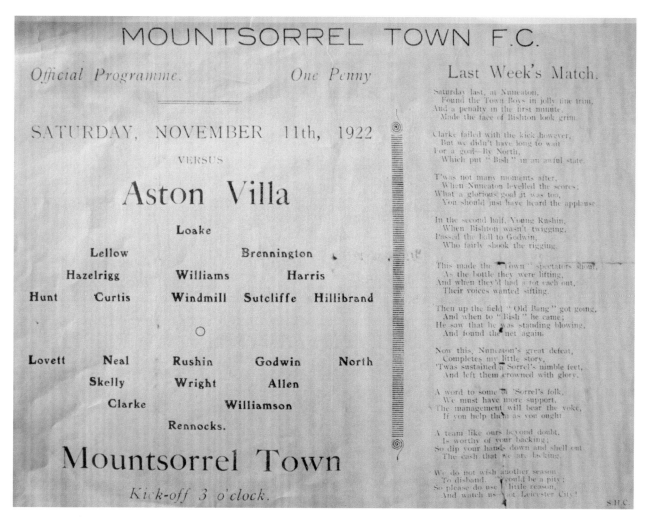

Mountsorrel Town football programme 11/11/22 (Armistice Day), image courtesy of Patrick Neal

Mountsorrel Granite Company laboratory, image courtesy of Lafarge

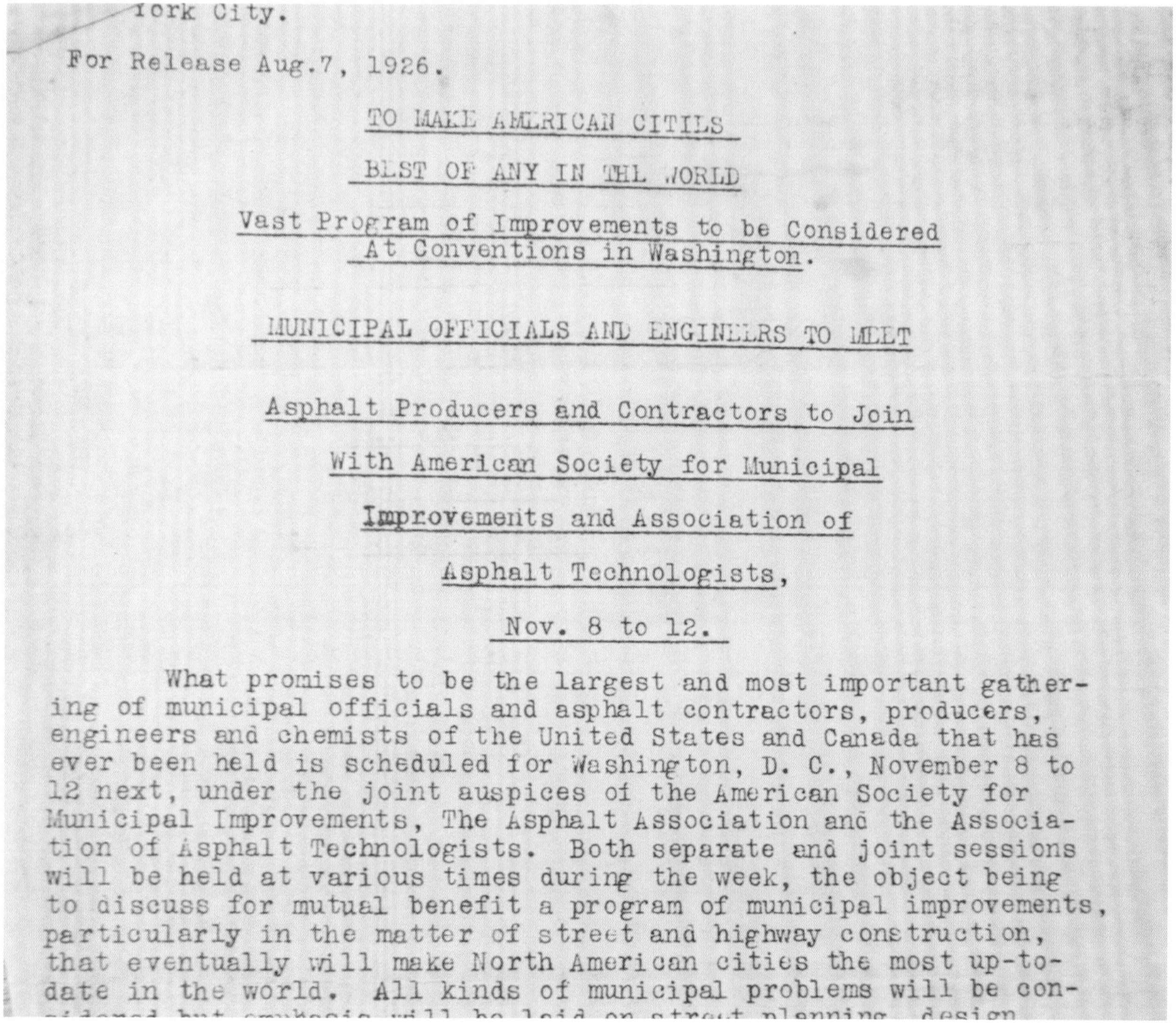

York City.

For Release Aug.7, 1926.

TO MAKE AMERICAN CITIES

BEST OF ANY IN THE WORLD

Vast Program of Improvements to be Considered
At Conventions in Washington.

MUNICIPAL OFFICIALS AND ENGINEERS TO MEET

Asphalt Producers and Contractors to Join

With American Society for Municipal

Improvements and Association of

Asphalt Technologists,

Nov. 8 to 12.

What promises to be the largest and most important gathering of municipal officials and asphalt contractors, producers, engineers and chemists of the United States and Canada that has ever been held is scheduled for Washington, D. C., November 8 to 12 next, under the joint auspices of the American Society for Municipal Improvements, The Asphalt Association and the Association of Asphalt Technologists. Both separate and joint sessions will be held at various times during the week, the object being to discuss for mutual benefit a program of municipal improvements, particularly in the matter of street and highway construction, that eventually will make North American cities the most up-to-date in the world. All kinds of municipal problems will be con-

The Asphalt Association press release 7th Augst 1926, image courtesy of Lafarge

MOUNTSORREL

GRANITE COY

LIMITED

Working Life

Mountsorrel Granite Company plaque, Cora Glasser, 2012

'It was called the Granite Boot Company and I started work there making men's boots and shoes, the quarry boots, they were called Bellers at the time...'

Margaret Manning (Nee Burton)

I went in a florist shop for a start off, then I worked for my dad for quite a long time, until they sold up, then I went to C&A's for a couple of years and then I went into a youth hostel and helped there for a season and then I went to the Cotswold and went waiting on in a posh hotel, which was nice. You can't beat sticking your feet under somebody else's table because all the money you get in your hand is yours to spend; you get your clothes provided (well mostly you do) and it was good.

Maureen Henson

It was called the Granite Boot Company actually and I started work there making men's boots and shoes, the quarry boots, they were called Bellers at the time, I can remember the name of them, I'll never forget, and I used to do them and in them days you used to have a doctor come round to all the factories to see, well, more or less, to see if you were good enough for the job, strong enough. Anyway I had to leave because I'd had rheumatic fever when I was 10 and I wasn't strong enough to do the job so

I had to leave. And I got a job at Lawson, you know Newbold & Burton's in Sileby, I started to make ladies' shoes. And then I finished there and came back to Mountsorrel, got married had the children and when I finally went back to work I went to work at Morris Shoes and I worked there for 28 years. It was down where the Parish Rooms are down the road.

Patrick Neal

I can't remember my first pay packet, I can remember my first pay packet at Rolls-Royce but I can't remember my first one at Morris's. I went as an apprentice and obviously the first day was things like going and getting measured up for your overalls and I can't even remember having a talk on health and safety in those days, you know, there was no such thing as health and safety. And we spent probably the first two or three days like in a classroom environment and then after that you spent three months in the factory and then three months at college, or thereabouts, and it was funny because after I left school and went to work at Morris's and subsequently at Rolls-Royce, I never failed one exam, I never passed one at school not one, I never even got an 'O' Level and yet when I went to work I passed everything that was in front of me.

Patricia Tomkins

No. Oh no, you didn't mention Rolls-Royce when you'd got all these quarrymen. Oh no. I'll tell you why, because, this might not be true but there again when we were all children of my age and we all wanted council houses, there wasn't a lot of council houses being built, but because they built the Rolls-Royce, well they altered Rolls-Royce and built more onto it, they had all the people from Derby come; where were they going to live? So they had a council estate for them, so we didn't get a look in, we just said, 'Oh, we're in a terraced house, three kids in one bedroom, two girls and boy, and the council houses are up there and people who've come from Derby got all these beautiful brand new council houses.' But I heard after that that no, they did Mountsorrel people in one, Derby in another, Mountsorrel in one, but all the people I could name

were all Derby. We didn't get a council house for three to four years, till the people that worked at the Rolls earned good money obviously and they started moving out, buying their own houses, and we ended up living in council houses for more or less the rest of my childhood, up to I was 18. My mum only just moved out of one about ten years ago, she moved out 'cause she was a widow and gave it up for other people, you know, with children. They come and ask you would you move out.

Our relations in Mountsorrel was all quarry, that was the work. There was not a lot to do unless you happened to own a shop, but I mean you can see photographs of all the men and all with the big moustaches. They used to grow a moustache to stop the dust going up their nose and they all sat there and they're all quarry you see, so there was the quarry. My dad was a lorry driver and he used to take the ballast. In 1953 when the floods came up, they came down the channel, didn't they, and expanded across England, Holland and all down the coast, and my dad, every day for I don't know

Aggregate freight transport, loading point at the main line terminal at Barrow-upon-Soar, image courtesy of Patricia Tomkins

how long, took ballasts from the quarry to Skegness and Stanton to bridge the gap where the water had come over. And I was talking to a friend's husband a few years ago and I mentioned this. He said, 'Do you know,' he says, 'My dad used to do that and he worked at Bardon Quarry.' So he was doing that at the same time but it was mostly quarry, that sort of people, say three-quarters were quarry workers.

Well it became a bit high tech, you know this quarry over the back where I lived finished, they filled it up with vet's rubbish and doctor's, bags of hospital rubbish and a bit of a stink up 'cause things were going in there that yeah, we didn't think, we had a big Mountsorrel stink you know. It was an awful smell coming off that quarry. This was probably in the '70's and it was in the paper, the Mountsorrel stink it was called 'cause they were filling the quarry up with rubbish and dustbin stuff and of course we were getting it more because I lived, I could have walked in a straight line and I could have been in the quarry hole. And when we first got married my bath was full of about a quarter of an inch of dust

but you didn't care, that's it, you'd put up with it. The men were at work, it was a quarry, there were dust and what do you expect?

My Dad did a lot of years at the quarry, but he did break it because he left, I don't know whether there was a bit of upset. I mean he didn't damage the lorry but I think there was something happened. All the granite was going out of a chute into the truck and my dad was standing in the truck with a spade, making it level. Well it kept going, didn't it? And it was filling up and it was up to my dad's waist and he was shouting and the noise of the train, the noise of the lorries, they couldn't hear him, and it were going up and up and up and he didn't know what to do. And he just managed to get his arm out and he took his cap off and he threw his cap at a lorry, at a lorry's rear mirror, and the bloke had to see this come out and he thought what's that? And then he looked and realised my dad was stuck in this and it was going up and up and up. And they stopped and of course got him out. But you imagine the weight of that granite.

And he used to go off with his billycan swinging on his little bag for his cup of tea. And he worked in what you call an hopper, so when you go up the top, The Navins, over the top into the quarry, and there's photographs, there's a big, big, and it's like the Tower of Babel, big thing and my dad used to be at the bottom and he used to sort the stone out. So the stone used to come bobbling along on a rubber belt, go up into this hopper and somehow get sort of sorted out somehow and it used to drop, and my dad used to sort of make sure it was clear.

And we'd go up and he'd get his tin of sweets out for us and we'd have a drop of tea out his billycan, and that used to happen quite often, at least twice a week. Now my brother, my younger brother, no my next brother, he worked in the other side of this path. You see there's a lot of paths that you could walk through but you had to mind the lorries because the lorries would be whizzing by with all the granite. But it was proper right of way. And my brother would be that other side and we'd shout, 'Ay-up David' and he'd come out and he'd wave.

Michael Griffiths

There was a postmaster in charge, called Harold Newman, and about four regular post persons. Some of these drove post vans for bulkier deliveries. The Post Office was a large and complex organisation but mail for the village was still sorted at the office there (mail posted in the village addressed to places in the village and elsewhere, and mail coming from outside). Some was stamped by hand with a Mountsorrel postmark. The post office stored parcels for collection and delivery, received and sent telegrams and operated the sale of stamps, official forms, postal orders, National Savings Bank, licences, stationery. It was the point of contact for many forms of payment and government services.

There was a very big range of workplaces in the village: Rolls-Royce, Clarke's Boxes, a leatherboard mill, a laundry, the quarry, a tarmacadam plant, the council roads depot, a flower nursery, Granite Boot Co, Glenfrith hospital, at least one small engineering firm. A lot of service industries: Co-op and other grocers of various sizes, hardware, electrical, pubs,

Working in a Mountsorrel factory, image courtesy of Patricia Tomkins

Worker's poem 1988, image courtesy of Patricia Tomkins

watchmaker, cobbler, bike shop, market garden, accommodation of several sorts, boatyard, schools, doctors, plumbers, builders, carpenters, car hire, builders, hairdressers, barbers, bakers, butchers, churches, a bus company, a transport café, chip shops, chemist, cinema, a commercial artist.

Janet Smith
We came to Mountsorrel when we got married as we could just about afford a new house in 1966.

When my son was a baby I talked to an old gentleman who told me that there was a tunnel that ran from the castle mound up to, what is now, Wood Lane/Swithland Lane. I was also talking to another old gentleman who remembered coming on the canal with his family for his father to work at the quarry.

I worked at Mountsorrel Hospital from 1980 until it closed in 1994. First as a Store Keeper/Clerk when my 'helper' was one of the residents and the only way of transporting all the heavy stores was a cardboard box on wheels (no health and safety!). I was told by the retiring Hospital Secretary (he came in 1946 at the beginning of the health service) that in the days of the workhouse (which was its original function) for travellers to get a bed for the night they had to break up a certain amount of Mountsorrel Granite into pieces that would fit through a certain sized hole. I was also told that many of the records of the hospital and memorabilia from its workhouse days had gone into the foundations of the day centre! There was one remaining record book, which, when the hospital closed, I sent to The Records Office.

It was an important part of the village when we came here in 1966. You would regularly see the residents out on a supervised walk. It was known in 1966 as an Asylum (which means refuge) but there were women who had been committed purely because they had had an illegitimate child or were 'wayward'.

The hospital had a complete life of its own.

Alan Smith

I worked at RollsRoyce from 1969-1971, when I was made redundant, and then 1978-2000, when I retired. There was a great camaraderie and many clubs. If you had a hobby they would start a club for you. I belonged to the Archery and Photographic clubs. Our children really enjoyed the Christmas parties with lots of great presents. It was a very sad day in 1994 when the Mountsorrel site closed completely. Houses have now been built on the site. One felt proud to say that you worked for Rolls-Royce.

'Rolls-Royce was a great community as far as I remember. It provided a lot of jobs, a very wide range of jobs, from shop floor workers to scientists and draftsmen, managers, all sorts of things. And they provided a lot of social events and welfare support for the workers.'

Betty Berger

The blasting used to start at half past eight in the morning at the quarry and that was the men's breakfast. Now they had a sort of, it wasn't a canteen as such but it was a shed-like building and there was a chap in there who, he was an old gentleman who'd worked at the quarry, he used to cook the breakfast and the men who came from Quorn and Rothley brought their breakfast with them. Now my grandpa always came home for his breakfast but my friend who lived next door to my grandma, we went to school together and her father stayed at the quarry for his breakfast. So sometimes if her big brother and sister wouldn't do it we used to take his breakfast for him and we used to go up with a, you know one of these like fishing creel things, they put a thing for the top and his breakfast was in there and we used to carry it up the lane under the bridges and round to the quarry.

All the factories they used to be going home on their bikes or walking or whatever and then we used to run back to school for half past one and then we had to go home at night as well so it was quite a lot of tracking about. We used to go up through the village by the Butter Market and over the hill up to school, until I moved down to the other school when I was eight and it wasn't so far to walk.

I'm interested in things like how the Martins came to take over the quarries in the 1840s because the chap was riding back, he worked for, I can't remember who he worked for now, some wealthy family, he was their land agent and he was riding back down by where Buddon Wood is now and the men were sitting on the side of the road that should have been working in the quarry and they said they hadn't had any work for about three weeks and they hadn't been paid and so on, and things were obviously falling apart. And so they took steps and they took over the franchise of the quarry and they started off that, so that was fascinating 'cause of course all through my childhood the Martins lived here and they lived up at the top of the hill there, what's now the old people's home where Sir Robert Martin and his brother came there when they first came to Mountsorrel. It's just

Workers laying roadstone from the Mountsorrel quarry, image courtesy of Lafarge

FATAL ACCIDENT AT THE QUARRIES. — An inquest on the body of James Harper, who died on Sunday from the effects of an accident in the quarries, was held on Tuesday morning at the Cottage Hospital, Mountsorrel, before Mr. Coroner Deane. —Captain Armstrong, her Majesty's inspector of factories, attended the inquiry. —John Harper said his father was 59 years of age, and employed as a random maker at the quarries. He saw him on Saturday after the accident, when deceased said he was helping to push a waggon, and did not see the post until it was too late. Deceased added that if he had not held himself up to the waggon he should have been cut to pieces.—Herbert Perkins, engine-fitter at the quarries, said that on Thursday morning he was working with Amos Freer in the engine shed. There was a coal truck in the shed, and deceased with others helped witness to move it out of the shed. Deceased was on the same side of the truck as witness. The truck door was hanging down, and as they passed out of the engine-house witness saw deceased crushed between the truck and the pillar of the door. Deceased was rolled round, and then fell down.—Amos Freer corroborated.—Dr. Skipworth, of Mountsorrel, said six of deceased's ribs were broken, and had penetrated to the lung. The ribs on the right side were quite driven in, and did not return to their proper place. He was of opinion that the ribs had been crushed in by the door. Deceased told him no one was to blame, and he gradually sank until Sunday, when death ensued.—The jury returned a verdict of accidental death.

Newspaper cutting from Loughborough Herald 17th October 1889, image courtesy of Sue Selfe

up there where you go up the little path at the side of those cottages and there's a house up there called The Poplars and it's now an old people's home but that was built for, the quarry manager lived there and then the Martins came back. Sir Robert Martin's father had been working up in the North of England. He was an engineer to do with collieries and things and then he came back and he was in charge of the quarries here. So they came and lived at The Poplars and then they bought the house at Woodhouse so then went and moved there.

Claris Wignall

Most of the men worked at the quarry and then there was two shoe factories, Smith's, that was down the little lane, and the other one was up Marsh Road. And then there was what they call the German Factory, some Germans, that was an elastic webbing factory similar to Wright's on a smaller scale, that was up Halstead Road. It was, well all of different sorts of webbing and that, but they didn't do the army work and then of course in later time it was Clarke's Box Factory. They started in a little place next to

Allens Garage and then they had the new factory built, but then during the war the Alvis works came from Coventry and took over the Clarke's Factory and then of course the Rolls-Royce, they came. 'Cause the link between the quarry were those big industries, those factories as it were, used to do a lot for their staff whether they be social events. At the Rolls I think they used to do quite a bit but I wasn't very much, you know, involved. It made a difference to Mountsorrel of course to have a place like that.

George Phillipson

Well the mineral is all owned, or was all owned, by the Earl of Lanesborough who, it's an Irish peerage and I don't know who owns it now because perhaps his daughter, who died 10 years ago or something like that and he had a daughter by his first marriage and so presumably she is landlord as it were and the Martin family in I think it's 1842 took on the lease of the quarry from the Lanesborough estate or whatever and the Martin family then built it up and continued with it right up until, I'm not sure but I guess when they amalgamated with Enderby and

Stoney Stanton. Then they went public and Redland bought them at that stage and the Martin family's connection disappeared.

Linda Tyman

Rolls-Royce was a great community as far as I remember. It provided a lot of jobs, a very wide range of jobs, from shop floor workers to scientists and draftsmen, managers, all sorts of things. And they provided a lot of social events and welfare support for the workers.

In the factory canteen, when I was a child, we used to have Christmas parties there, every year, which I remember quite vividly. In 1959 the factory burnt down and was rebuilt and as part of the rebuilding, or a few years after that, they built a new canteen and social building which was on Mountsorrel Lane, going towards Rothley. And that was used for dances and all sorts of entertainment and it was a great facility for the village because outsiders were allowed to go as well so it brought a lot of people together.

My grandfather worked for the Alvis company and that was the reason why he and his family moved to Mountsorrel because in 1940 in the blitz the Alvis factory in Coventry was bombed and they transferred early in 1941 to premises on Linkfield Road in Mountsorrel. At the time it was known as Clarke's Box Factory but it was requisitioned by the government although they'd made cars and aero parts in Coventry they were to make aeroplane parts for the war effort. I think it was probably the only suitable place in the village at that time and Clarke's Boxes, they transferred to Anstey and Rothley and Shepshed I think, for the time when their factory was in use by Alvis.

A lot of the men that came from Coventry had to lodge with local families and they started work at 8 o'clock and finished at 6 and also on Saturday mornings. But a lot of them went back to Coventry after the shift finished on Saturday and they were allowed to come back a bit late on Monday morning because the first bus from Coventry didn't get here in time to start the 8 o'clock shift.

Mon. 4.8.86.

A Week in the lives of
five Warehouse Ladies

As usual the day starts with Morris
"Good Mornings". By 2pm no charge. "bu
the sun came out and Rose came
with the "Mablethorpe" rock. Handsome
box man came we unloaded van no
chit chat this time. Day ended.
peacefully.

Tues 5.8.86.

Usual "Good Mornings". Jean eating
every thing in sight. Morning grey
with sunny spells. Winnie won a
share in the football and we had
two toffees. Boxes unloaded wrong
ones. Day ended peacefully.

Wed. 6.8.86.

Bad start to the morning Morris "agro
Weather blustery. looks like rain
Jenny came round with two toffees won th
other half of football. Recieved your

'ard today. Morris worried when you
said you'd have another week off.
Tea time we had a treat? ""
My word 3.30 laughter "Baby Talk."
Interesting conversation on "DRAINS"

Thurs. 7.8.86.

Weather Windy grey miserable. Sad
news Jean broke the flask. Hurray its
Pay Day Pauline brought the AVON
More boxes delivered very talkative.
used to live on Boundary Rd.
Day ended uneventful.

FRI. 8.8.86.
Well Friday again smashing
Tina has lost 8lb she's over the
moon. Chris had an operation on
his finger performed by Nurse
Beverley. Weather grey & cold.

THE END.

Not a very exciting week.

Diary extracts August 1986, image courtesy of Patricia Tomkins

But then a lot of people actually moved here. My grandfather moved his family here, all the family rather than him commuting between here and Coventry. And the factory made parts for the Rolls-Royce Merlin and Kestrel engines and after a while the production increased and they built another factory which they called it Alvis Number Two; it was behind the existing one and it was near the pond which had been formerly a brickworks.

The person who started the Granite Boot Company, he was called James Smith, must have realised that there was a good market for the sort of things they were producing, there'd be a ready clientele of people. It changed its name over the years; it became Morris's for many years. And I believe there was Parker's Boot and Shoe Factory in Linkfield road.

There were a family called the Baum family and there was Edgar Baum, he had a nursery on Rothley Road and then there were three Baum brothers who had gardens on Boundary Road and Halstead Road. They would grow plants, they would grow tomatoes and things and sell them at the appropriate time of year.

There was another one on Halstead Road run by a man called Peter Bowie and eventually he sold that and I live on the housing development where he used to run his business. And the original bungalow that he lived in is at the back of our house.

And one of the biggest ones was on Cross Lane, it was called Rowena Nurseries. I think when the Baums started it was 30s, 40s time. Rowena Nurseries started in the 1960s I believe by the Carpenter family. I used to work there when I was about 15, used to on a Saturday or when they were busy and cart barrow loads of soil about. It was hard work but it was quite a laugh, really. And they developed their business quite rapidly and they moved across the road on Cross Lane and then eventually they moved up to Wyevale Garden Centre near the Rothley Lodge and that became Rowena Nurseries, so they moved there just before the bypass was built.

And a lot of local women used to work there at certain times of the year when they were planting out seedlings and stuff. My mum worked there and it was quite a popular place to work because you could fit it into school hours and that sort of thing, so that was one of the places that provided a lot of employment on a seasonal basis.

Mary Neal

We used to go dancing there at the Rolls-Royce Canteen. It was really good, we used to really enjoy it but the only thing was we didn't go Christmas Eve because that was family time but we always went New Year's Eve and between Christmas and New Year. It was The Canteen that we used to have the dances at and because it had been shut up, the floor of course, they got the heating on and it had been very, very cold and the floor consequently got very wet and I can remember once I had a white dress on and all around the bottom of my dress was like this brown at the end of the night, it was all brown round the bottom. I think it was polish, the polish off the floor!

LLoyd Tomlyn

The Morriss Laundry from Cyprus Road, Aylestone, Leicester came to No. 14 in August 1937 after amalgamating with the Belvoir Laundry from Belvoir Drive, Aylestone, Leicester owned by Tom Bettany, though he soon relinquished his partnership. The name Morriss was Olive Cooper's maiden name. Before they came here, in the 20th Century the premises had a number of owners and various uses including a Brewery, a Jam factory, a Cinema and a dye works. At some stage, probably when the dye works were there, a large Lancashire boiler and steam engine had been installed, probably around 1923. It was these items which attracted Mr Cooper there as the laundry would require plenty of steam for driving the steam engine and the exhaust from which was used to make the hot water. There was also a 3,000 gallon water storage tank on the flat roof. It certainly wasn't the living accommodation at the front, which had been condemned and had to be refurbished. There wasn't any 3-phase electric power on the premises. This came later when the first two electric motors were used, first to drive part

Mary Crawley loading Armstrong drying tumblers at Morriss Laundry, image courtesy of Lloyd Tomlyn

Some of the ladies on the staff at Morriss Laundry in the 1950's, image courtesy of Lloyd Tomlyn

of the drive shafting and a fan for the drying room. As time moved on and the extension was built, the steam engine was then past its best and everything was then electrically powered.

By the time the laundry closed there were around 60 or 70 motors on the premises. Most of the machines then had their own electric motor. The large drying tumblers each had two. The business had also started to do dry cleaning and the Spencer dry cleaning machine had about 8 motors on it, operating pumps, valves and drain valves as well as the drum itself.

Unfortunately I cannot find any photographs of the place before the extensions in 1950 which were built when Mr Cooper bought the Mill House next door and its premises in 1948 including the old Water Mill. This had been built in 1765 and ran through to 1912 when it was closed. There was an attempt to sell it, but this wasn't successful. It remained untouched until the start of World War II when all the machinery and most of the timberwork were commandeered for the war effort. I believe the

timber was used to make moulds for producing bulletproof aircraft fuel tanks, possibly in the old factory in Boundary Road Mountsorrel.

From the time of constructing the Mountsorrel lock in the early 1800's, when the River Soar was canalised, compensation of £12.10s (£12.50) per annum had been paid to the Mill owners for the loss of water, up to the time the Mill was closed.

I don't think there were particularly thoughts at that time of trying to be green when the laundry steam engine exhaust was used to make hot water, it was just more efficient and money saving. The same would apply after Mr Cooper attempted to generate electricity from the waterwheels of the old Mill. It was just that there were continuous power cuts after the war and this might help. However after a lot of planning and the recommendation by a consulting engineer to remove the old waterwheel and replace it with a modem water turbine, an inspector came from the Trent River Board to say that if it were to go ahead they would charge for the water even though it was running through the wheel channel anyway. Just the opposite of what had happened until 1912. The charge for the water would be more than the value of the electricity produced. This was estimated to be around 9kW for 24 hours a day. So the scheme was abandoned. It might be very different today but the Mill has gone and a flood weir stands in its place, after a compulsory purchase order by the then Trent River Board. Its present owners are The Environment Agency.

The brick-built factory beyond the Marine Centre were the premises of the leather board manufacturers Paulson and Paulson. They would take in the scrap leather from boot and shoe manufactures in Leicester and Northampton. It was then ground up and mixed with water. This emulsion was then pressed in what looked like an original hand-operated wine press. This created a board about 2' by 3' which would be stacked in layers of about 20, interleaved with felt sheets and placed in a more powerful hydraulic press. After removing most of the water, these were then hung in heated drying rooms. These boards

could then be reused as insoles and interlayers of new shoes. The felt sheets would be taken to the laundry about once a month for cleaning. Another customer for the laundry.

As this trade gradually subsided after the closure of many shoe manufacturers and the introduction of alternative materials, and with cheaper products from abroad, Paulson and Paulson started to produce hosiery. It was at this time that the two storey building at the rear caught fire and it was reduced to a single storey. This business eventually also closed. It is now Newtons4th, an IT business. Beyond this factory were the premises of Noel Wakeling for car repairs.

After the laundry closed and the machinery was auctioned off in 1960, including the boiler, which was the reason for Mr Cooper moving here in the first place, the house at No.14 and some of the outbuildings were demolished and the main building was made into a showroom and offices for the sale and servicing of boats and outboard motors.

Aerial shot of the Marine Centre with Paulson & Paulson factory behind, image courtesy of Lloyd Tomlyn

It was called Mountsorrel Marine Centre. This was a completely new venture for Mr Cooper, who would continue running it until he retired at the age of 70. I remained as one of only three of the staff he kept on, but jobs were found for most of the other workers. The other two to remain were Dave Squires and Dorothy Smith.

The Mountsorrel Marine Centre was run quite successfully until Mr Cooper's retirement when it was sold to The Ladyline Group based in Market Drayton. I continued working for Ladyline as Group Service Manager for two years, but after a disagreement over no investments and lack of progress, started my own business next door, Lloyd Tomlyn, in the same trade. A few years later the Ladyline Group went bankrupt and the main part of the premises was sub-leased to Butler Reynolds, for the sale and service of construction plant. It was during this break that I was able to lease the end part of the premises for a showroom for boats and outboards. They remained here until 1992 when the lease they had taken over from Ladyline ran out

and they moved to their own premises in Costock. By then I had also retired and the property stood empty for 2 years due to a controversy with the Borough planners. This resolved, it was then leased to Charnwood and Highmeres, dealers and service engineers in horticultural machinery, who are still here.

Closed Morriss Laundry buildings, ready to be converted to the Mountsorrel Marine Centre, image courtesy of Lloyd Tomlyn

Inside Morriss Laundry (note Military overalls bottom right - Army & RAF provided a lot of business), image courtesy of Lloyd Tomlyn

'...he used to have to put the dynamite in, they used to drill 'oles because they didn't have machinery then and they used to have to swing down on a rope, put the dynamite in and then go back up.'

Betty Berger

You got paid a lot more if you were at Rolls-Royce and we lost several labourers who said, 'They've offered me a lot more to go and work at Rolls-Royce', so that had an impact on local businesses I suppose as well. And then of course all the way along the street there were shops. As you've probably found out already there were lots of shops, lots of grocery shops and all sorts, you know everything. Butcher shops there were, one, two, three, four, four butchers shops in the main that I remember and then they used to come round with a van as well and deliver the meat. I don't know how it ever stayed fresh 'cause they used to come round. And the Co-op had, we were very excited after the war began 'cause they had one of these electric floats and this little chap used to come round and deliver the milk with it instead of horse and cart you know. And the coal used to come on a horse and cart of course and the bread, they had a proper thing that they brought round with the bread and things, you know. So all these things were, before the war and during the war, brought round like that because there was no other way to do it.

Down the road here there was a little sweet shop on the corner where, there's buildings there now but it was an old cemetery there, nearly opposite to Watling Street and the Butter Market. It was an old cemetery and it had next to it a very old building which is long gone and the cemetery was there because the people who owned the building, the blacksmith was there when I was a child and my father used to work for them and they used mend tools for him and things.

Jackie Loughlin

[My father did] a bit of this and a bit of that. In actual fact he used to get injured quite a bit because he used to have to put the dynamite in [at the quarry], they used to drill 'oles because they didn't have machinery then and they used to have to swing down on a rope, put the dynamite in and then go back up. Or sometimes put it in and run kind of thing, when they blasted. He worked there quite a long while though. And I can remember sitting out on the wall waiting for him to come home at dinner, it must have been about 50 years, it must have been. A long while. And I can remember coming home from school, as I say it was a longish while, one day and I says to me mam, 'Where's me dad?' She says, 'In a hospital.' So he'd obviously been injured that time. But then he progressed, he got better, he had angina, so he had to have a lighter job and he used to go round doing the gardens for the managers and he used to do it up Watling Street where the school was, St. Peter's. It's an old people's home now. And then he used to do all the fences up for the quarry round the old quarry, now it's a landfill site. Well it's not now because they've filled it in. He used to have to check all the fences round there.

I left school when I was 15, went for an interview there and it were Madge Davey then her name was, the floor lady. And my first day was on the Friday I think when I started on the Monday and I went on wire stitching, what were called wire stitching and they were shoe boxes and you used to have to put wire stitches in it. I did that but then I progressed through it until I was on the big machines and we used to do all the shoe boxes for all the things, you know, shoe places around because there was lots.

And Newbold's and Burton's, Stead & Simpson's, School Boot that was in Sorrell then we used to do Airfix boxes for the aeroplanes.

You did the same thing. Well no, not always, well I did 'cause I went on automatic machine and I did that every day. I walked out once because the machine went wrong and you're on piecework you see and George, that were another mechanic, he was the head mechanic, he got it on him an' all, and he wouldn't come and look at my machine. So I says to him, 'If you don't come and look at my machine, I'm going home.' He says, 'Well I'm not coming.' So I says, 'Right then I'm going home.' So I'm walking out and the manager, Mr Brown, was running after me, 'Don't go, don't go because I've got nobody else.' I said, 'I'm going.' because then you could just walk in a job and walk out.

Kay Valentine (Nee Porter)
Oh gosh yes I worked at Rolls-Royce myself for a while. It was about 12 months I think and I used to work in the crack testing department and I used

to do all the paperwork as the chaps had to test the engine parts for the cracks, I used to have to do all the paperwork for them. And again you see that was another place that used to organise a lot for the village, they used to do fetes and things like that so as I say I was only there a year. But a lot of people that I grew up with obviously worked at Rolls-Royce and still do really out at Derby. I also worked at the Mountsorrel Elastic Factory when I first left school, that was in Halstead Road. And I started there on the Monday after I left school on the Friday in 1965 and I was office junior and it was fabulous, I learnt so much from them. German people that owned it, and they were wonderful, they used to take us out at Christmas and treat us to a Christmas meal and bought us presents and of course the elastic went all over, it used to go to Derby and Nottingham and everywhere you see to make corsets, that was the main aim of it.

Maureen Henson

I remember Paulson & Paulson's down the village, it's down opposite where we used to have a fish shop down at the bottom, Dockery's and opposite there was a shop called Proud's and down that yard was a mill and my dad used to work down there and it used to be the leather board makers and they used to get all the old mush of leather and it was all soaked in water. And they'd got like big moulds, I've seen them do it, it was these really big, square moulds and they used to get all this mush with the water and that and it used to fill up and then they'd sort of shake it like mad and then it used to be pressed down into leather boards, big presses come down and pressed it into leather boards. My Dad he worked there, gosh, I was only a youngster, I can't remember when it closed down, it did close down. I should think I'd be about what, 12, 13, but I can always remember him going down the mill and going down at night to lock everywhere up, I can remember him taking this little Jack Russell with him because she used to shake the rats. It were always full of rats every morning. Well they would, it's out on the river you see and the rats used to come in and he'd shake them, oh gosh.

Broad Hill quarry, image courtesy of Lafarge

JW Porter & Son Haulage Contractors, image courtesy of Kay Valentine (Nee Porter)

Robin Davies

My dad worked at the quarry yes, before the War when times were hard. I think he was just a general labourer, I recall one or two stories about how hard they had to work there. One story he did tell me that he was working emptying wagons by hand shovelling the ballast out or whatever it was by hand and there was a gang of them working in the trucks and a manager came by and watched this man work and he said, 'How much are you paying that man an hour to work and shovel this out?' because he was faster than anybody else with a shovel. And I forget what the figure was thruppence an hour or something silly like that, and he said, 'Well that's no good, cut it in half and…' and apparently that's how it was in the '30s, really hard. And then I always remember he was telling me how they used to shunt the wagons round, they used to use ash poles to stick through the wheels to make them brake because the wheels were turning round and they used to jam.

Patrick Neal

I can't remember my first pay day as such but I certainly can remember leaving Morris's and I can remember exactly what happened there. I'd had a row with the gaffer at Morris's and I thought, 'Oh I'm fed up with this,' and I went up to Rolls-Royce and I said, 'Have you got any jobs?' They said, 'We think so, would you like to come for an interview?' I went for the interview. It was 1966, May because we got married in September of '66 and I can remember having the interview and I'm sure it was a Thursday because I went back and I remember going into

Loughborough and the market was on and before I went back into work at Morris's in the afternoon I remember I went to the little Chinese and had one of these business lunches upstairs in a Chinese restaurant. I came home and the Saturday morning there was a knock on the door, and as I say I lived at No. 45 and this first house past the Youth Café here, a guy called Eric Giles used to live there and he was the personnel manager. I was still in bed and he came knocking on my door on the Saturday morning with an envelope and my mum come running upstairs she said, 'Oh there's an envelope here for you from Rolls-Royce,' and it was the offer of the job. I went in on Monday, handed my notice in and started the following Monday at Rolls-Royce. I went in as a MOD investigation engineer, I was investigating the changes to the aircraft engines when they wanted to say, 'We don't want that knob there, we want it there.' I'd have a look and see how long it would take us and what we needed to do to bring it in. And I can remember when I left Morris's my wages were £15 a week and I went up to Rolls-Royce and it was £17.50 a week and to me that was the earth 'cause in those days once you could, if you could make £1,000 a year, I always remember somebody saying to me, 'Do you know some of the people at Rolls-Royce are on £1,000 a year,' and I thought, 'God that's the earth!' I mean I can't remember what our mortgage was but our mortgage must have been something like £17 a month and to us that was a lot of money then. So then I went to Rolls-Royce and I stayed at Rolls-Royce in Mountsorrel until 1984 and then I moved to Derby in 1984 at Rolls-Royce and I was there until 2000.

I liked the people at Rolls-Royce very much. I liked the fun and the times we had and in fact I always said for years and years the only way I was coming out of Rolls-Royce was feet first. And if they were to cut me open, it would be Rolls-Royce through, like a stick of rock, but towards the end they were bringing all the graduates in and they wanted to sit on computers all day, they didn't want to go out and look at what was happening on the shop floor so I got out when I was 57, 58 when I left but I loved Rolls-Royce, I loved it.

The other thing I was going to say, when I worked at Morris's we used to bike in, about four or five of us used to bike in every morning. There was Mary's father, myself and a couple of other blokes and we used to bike in every morning and the working week was half past seven until five every day and half past seven until twelve on a Saturday morning and that was the working week. And then when they started to drop it down a bit you could only work overtime at weekends if you'd worked overtime in the week and if you were two minutes late in the morning you just didn't get any overtime and they'd stop you quarter of an hour's pay if you were two minutes late.

Noel Wakeling

I think it's always a bit disconcerting for anybody with their first day at work although there were one or two men, or certainly people older than myself, that I knew, so it wasn't as bad as what you might have imagined it to be, but I did enjoy the mechanical side, the repairs and that, and of course in those days the firm that I was working for, Gillett's Garage, they were Ford agents but they didn't just repair cars they

SPECIAL CHARACTERISTICS

OF

𝕸𝖔𝖚𝖓𝖙𝖘𝖔𝖗𝖗𝖊𝖑 𝕲𝖗𝖆𝖓𝖎𝖙𝖊 𝕸𝖆𝖈𝖆𝖉𝖆𝖒

IN RESPECT OF WHICH

It is Superior to all other Roadstones in the English Market.

1.—It is better in colour.

2.—It is more uniformly broken.

3.—It is more equal in wear.

4.—It dries more quickly after rain.

5.—It is cleaner, being less muddy in wet weather and less dusty in dry.

6.—Its binding properties are greater.

7.—It makes the roads more quickly.

8.—It makes the roads more uniformly level and without lumps or loose stones.

9.—It is tougher and more difficult to break.

10.—It has a lower specific gravity—thus 100 tons of Mountsorrel Macadam will cover the same area as

103 tons 10 cwt. from Quenast.	107 tons 2 cwt. from Rowley.
104 ,, 7 ,, ,, Groby.	108 ,, 7 ,, ,, Guernsey.
106 ,, 6 ,, ,, Bardon Hill	109 ,, 13 ,, ,, Clee Hill.
106 ,, 9 ,, ,, Markfield.	110 ,, 7 ,, ,, Charnwood

111 tons 10 cwt. from Middleton in Teesdale.

did the whole of the Ford range of products, which were agricultural and heavy goods and cars, so they covered the whole spectrum and I did enjoy that, especially there were times, during the summertime more so than the winter time, when we used to have to go out onto a farm somewhere, it might be just outside Loughborough, it might be 20 miles away, but it was nice to have a trip out there and we might have to do the repair that it required while we were there or we might have to load it onto the trailer and bring it back to the workshop if the work was too extensive. But I enjoyed it. You'd get thrown at you quite a lot of jobs, I mean when I said I enjoyed it, I did enjoy it but there were many a job that you weren't so keen on especially on a Saturday morning when the whole of the workshop had to be cleaned and the whole of the workshop floor had to be scraped and cleaned with paraffin and then bags full of sawdust tipped down and brushed over and dried up so that it left the workshop nice and clean ready for starting Monday morning. That were one of the jobs that I wasn't so keen on and the other one was filling people up with fuel, whether it be petrol or

diesel, even in those days it was another job that you had to do or take your turn at doing but there was always something, a little job that probably wasn't as nice that you probably didn't enjoy it as much as you would have done doing other jobs. It never bothered me about getting my hands dirty and getting stuck into doing a repair, but of course you had to work with somebody so that you learnt the job properly, but there were certain people that you didn't enjoy working with everybody. I won't mention one particular chap, I didn't enjoy working with him but having said that I think that probably working with him stood me in good stead so you've got to take the rough with the smooth.

Your wages then were around about £2, just over £2 a week and out of that you had to have, you went to technical college for one day and one evening a week, of which the company would cover the cost of you being away for the day. There was one particular time when I did flout the rules and it stuck in my mind for ever and this was it. It was in the very, very early 1950's and the Ford V8 Pilot car was just being produced by Ford and we'd just had a new one delivered and it was stood in the road outside, that was in Greenclose Lane at Loughborough, and Gerald Potter was the managing director, was talking to the driver that had just delivered it. I was as you can imagine, I was only 16 and I backed a vehicle out of the workshop into Greenclose Lane, now I shouldn't have been in that vehicle because I hadn't got a driving licence and so apart from moving the vehicle in the workshop itself, I shouldn't have been in it, especially not to go onto the road. And I can remember reversing this vehicle across the road and backed it straight into this brand new car! So I got my ears chewed off for that, I didn't get the sack or anything like that but I did get my ears chewed off for it, but the thing was that saying about flouting the rules, that was one time I did and I shouldn't have been in that vehicle. So I did flout the rules and fortunately for me and fortunately for the firm, the only damage that it did to the new car and to the car I was in, was a slight dent on the bumper of the car I was in and the chromium hub cap on the wheel got a dent in it, that was all it did, but it was enough.

Angus Shedden

Without doubt the best thing about my job is the fact that every day is completely and utterly different, I have so much variety in what I do. I have to get involved in everything from the landscape that we work in, managing the Triple SI, looking after trees and plants and animals, to blasting and blowing things up, to big dump trucks and diggers, to managing quite complex accounts and the finances of the site, through to the bit which in many ways I really love, which is managing the people. With over 100 people working on site there's a huge amount that is actually about how you manage the people and because health and safety is so important in our industry, a lot of my time and a lot of my work goes into trying to ensure that people come to work safely, enjoy their work, and if they're working safely and enjoying what they do, then actually it will be a successful site. So that's without doubt the best thing about my job. The cons, there's probably two really, one is you're never going to get particularly rich and the second one is it can be really long hours so it's quite common to be in work at seven o'clock and often can be seven o'clock in the evening when you finish and weekends are quite regularly, in for weekends, so I've just got a young son who is one year old and so it can get a bit tough when you don't see him for a few days because he's always in bed by the time I get home and things. So yeah, that's probably the one downside but overall I love what I do.

George Phillipson

I mean my history at Redland is I joined Redland Roadstone as it was, as Production Director, and I think we had six quarries and then Redland Roadstone was amalgamated with Redland Gravel and Redland Readymix in about 1976 or something like that and I became a Regional Director running the West Midlands, but my office was at Wolverhampton so that was about two years or something. And then I came back as Joined or Assistant Managing Director or some such title and then I became Managing Director and I had a responsibility as well for France and then latterly North America and the Middle East and I became Redland Plc's Board Director with responsibility for

all Redland's quarrying activities in North America, UK, France and the Middle East. In our market area we were always the biggest because you need to be in the quarrying industry, you need to be the biggest really to get the benefits of scale and market strength and so on. So I sort of went from Production Director in Redland Roadstone to being the Chairman of the companies.

So I don't know what the highlight was, there were a lot of highlights! I think probably opening the new plant in 1974 because we'd started with a clean sheet of paper, it was designed in-house, we didn't do the drawings but everything was designed in-house with a small team; we had a couple of contract draftsmen and myself and we always had a meeting every Saturday morning, we met in the offices and had bacon butties and chewed the fat over as to the design and how it was moving forward and how did we solve this problem and so on.

But the great thing about the new plant at Mountsorrel, it was built or designed by quarrymen for quarrymen so one of the things we've always said to ourselves was, 'How do we change this when it breaks? Where do we need beings with lifting equipment and so on, how can we get at it without dismantling the whole plant?' So we then went out to tender and the contractors built it all to our design and it was certainly the first loader for loading the trucks, it was the first one I think in the world that was fully computerised and that was 1974 and I think it's probably still the benchmark of computerised load-out for trucks because it was further than that, you knew where the truck was, you knew when it was back in the quarry because you put in the travel time for the job and it kept stock for you and it's a super system.

Noel Wakeling

There is something that I've been quite pleased probably with myself, not connected to work as such but to the history of Mountsorrel. My uncle Bernard Jones who was the scoutmaster here, he was a lay preacher at St. Peter's church, generally a good egg. Unfortunately he slipped over, broke his neck and it paralysed him. During this time he wrote a book on Mountsorrel and it's called *The Story of Mountsorrel*. Now he became more and more infirm with his disability and he said to me, 'I would like you if you would take over all the slides, I'll give you the slide projector and all the details I've got together whilst compiling my book.' And he'd also written a lot of info down to each slide of which there were quite a lot, he used to go round to various places giving talks on Mountsorrel. And he said, 'Would you do the same?' Well I'd never done it before although I had been able to get up and do some public speaking but I'd never done anything like this before. And since then I've increased the collection of Mountsorrel slides I should think we've now got at the last count we've got about 330 slides on Mountsorrel itself and the info that we've gained between that, and I must say this, that it really has been one of the highlights of my older life that we've been able to do those talks and let people enjoy the older Mountsorrel and what it was like. Some of those photographs are extremely old so I think that that really is quite a highlight which I've enjoyed doing and still enjoy doing.

p 120 Mountsorrel Granite Company at the British Empire exhibition, London, image courtesy of Lafarge